CHOOSING & USING
Paints and Wallpapers

House Beautiful

CHOOSING & USING
Paints and Wallpapers

Jane Tidbury

Ebury Press
London

First published 1995
1 3 5 7 9 10 8 6 4 2

This edition published in 1995 by Ebury
Press, Random House,
20 Vauxhall Bridge Road, London
SW1V 2SA

Random House Australia (Pty) Limited,
20 Alfred Street,
Milsons Point, Sydney, New South
Wales 2061, Australia

Random House New Zealand Limited,
18 Poland Road, Glenfield,
Auckland 10, New Zealand

Random House South Africa (Pty)
Limited, PO Box 337, Bergvlei,
South Africa

Random House UK Limited
Reg. No. 954009

A CIP catalogue record for this book is
available from the
British Library.

ISBN 009 178942 7

Editor: Emma Callery
Designed by Jerry Goldie Graphic
Design London

Colour separations by Colorlito S.r.l.,
Milan

Printed and bound in Singapore by Tien
Wah Press

CONTENTS

INTRODUCTION   7

CHOOSING PAINTS AND WALLPAPERS   8
Planning your scheme   10
The right scheme for the right room   12
Working with colour   14
Working with pattern   16
Choosing paint   18
Decorative paint effects   21
Painted details   24
Choosing wallpapers   26
Floral designs   29
Small patterns   30
Traditional style   33
The finishing touch   35

USING PAINTS AND WALLPAPERS   36
Decorative paint effects   38
Sponging and ragging   40
Colour washing   42
Distressing   44
Crackle glaze   45
Marbling   46
Stencilling   48
Stripes and checks   50
Painted furniture   52
Painted floors   54
Painting textured wallcoverings   56
Wallpaper borders   58
Découpage   60

BASICS   62
Preparing surfaces for decoration   64
Painting   67
Wallpapering   71

Stockists and suppliers   76
Index   78
Acknowledgments   80

INTRODUCTION

Welcome to our *Choosing and Using* series of practical books. Every home-owner knows the problems that so often go with the pride in creating a comfortable and attractive place to live. So with this in mind, our clear guides have been created to form a useful and inspirational series to keep on hand while you choose and use the essential elements for every room. *Paints and Wallpapers*, for example, guides you through the maze of paint and wallpaper options. With practical advice and step-by-step instructions it also shows you how to create and achieve the professional results that are right for you and your home.

The other books in the series cover aspects in an equally detailed way and I know you'll find each book as useful and inspiring as every issue of *House Beautiful* magazine.

Pat Roberts Cairns
Editor

Left *A soft floral design of wallpaper contrasts strongly with the strong colour wash, but the toning colours make for a cohesive overall effect.*

CHOOSING PAINTS AND WALLPAPERS

Whether starting from scratch or revamping an existing scheme, you will probably find yourself faced with one of the main decorating dilemmas, what to do with the walls. Walls are the decorative backdrop to any room, and whether pale and subtle or bold and eye-catching, they help to balance and pull together all the elements of colour and pattern within it. If you're going back to square one, thinking about how to treat the walls should be part and parcel of drawing up creative ideas.

Paints and wallpapers are the essential materials for decorating. The key question is deciding when and where to use them. A coat of paint, for example, is one of the easiest ways to introduce instant colour to any room. Stunning results can be achieved with just paint alone, either plain or softly patterned as a decorative finish, or by combining gloss and matt textures in a scheme.

Wallpaper is used primarily for the pattern it brings to a room. It is also used for its colour possibilities, and the warmth and softness it can add to smooth plastered walls. Small and regular patterns lend a sense of order; whereas more obvious figurative and floral designs help to create a less formal atmosphere and add interest and richness. This is especially so where everything else in the room is plain. Papers can be chosen simply for the background haze of colour they provide or as a key part of the overall design of the room. Even when plain colours are preferred, embossed or textured papers make an attractive base for paint and can be used in a variety of ways to create distinctive design details.

Right Colour and pattern are the key ingredients to any scheme. Here a shade of paint has been picked from the small print wallpaper to create a charming and colourful theme for a bedroom.

PLANNING YOUR SCHEME:
Finding inspiration
Finding a style
Researching a style
Practical pointers

THE RIGHT SCHEME FOR THE RIGHT ROOM:
Size
Function
Existing furnishings

WORKING WITH COLOUR:
Choosing the colours
Colour moods
Playing safe with colour
Practical pointers

WORKING WITH PATTERN:
Setting the scene
Paint versus wallpaper
Practical pointers

CHOOSING PAINT:
Deciding on what you want
Types of paint
Newly plastered walls
What's what
Practical pointers

DECORATIVE PAINT EFFECTS:
Simple patterns
What's what
Practical pointers

PAINTED DETAILS:
Woodwork
Walls
Furniture

CHOOSING WALLPAPERS:
Assessing the design
What's what

FLORAL DESIGNS

SMALL PATTERNS:
Stripes
Paint effect wallpapers

TRADITIONAL STYLE:
Relief-pattern papers

THE FINISHING TOUCH:
Borders

PLANNING YOUR SCHEME

Planning a decorative scheme is about adding your own personality and style in a way that works well for the room you have in mind. It should balance and complement all the aspects - its size, function, furnishings and accessories - while leaving plenty of scope for creative ideas. The secret to successful decorating ideas is to allow yourself enough time to consider the options. It is always best to try to work on the room as a whole and to think through the entire scheme before make any final design decisions and purchases. If you feel unsure about using colour or pattern, careful planning will help you to develop design solutions and give you the confidence to follow them through.

FINDING INSPIRATION

Above *Coordinating wall-papers and borders make scheme planning even easier. Collect sample swatches of patterns you like, and use these to build up ideas for your decor before making a final decision.*

Few of us have the experience to visualise colours and schemes. Neither are we always that sure about the kind of mood and style we want to create in a specific room. The fun part of putting together a scheme is looking for ideas and inspiration that will not only guide you through the creative process but will help clarify your likes and dislikes. Postcards, magazines, a picture of a favourite painting, all show colour and pattern at work and can provide the spark of inspiration for your own scheme. It could be the smallest detail in a picture where two complementary shades suggest a combination you have never thought of before, or you may come across a complete room setting that sums up everything you want to achieve. Professional designers collect all kinds of bits and pieces that they store away as inspiration for future schemes. You could work in the same way by gathering a variety of images that appeal and starting your own visual notebook. As well as providing an invaluable colour reference when out shopping, pictured images of colour and design can be useful when trying to imagine how a particular shade will work in a room.

Try to broaden your creative search to more unusual sources. Nature abounds with examples of colour: a group of flowers in a vase can be a scheme in itself, the hues of an autumnal landscape reveal how subtle combinations can work together. Images from foreign parts can be equally stimulating, challenging the accepted convention of colour and pattern. Think about the fresh simplicity of Mediterranean houses of stark white and bright blue, or the exuberant richness of the orient.

Most suppliers and shops provide sample swatches of paint

colours and wallpapers. Collect any that you find attractive as you browse and add these to your notebook. Having gathered together a range of ideas and images you can then begin to think about the kind of decorative style you wish to create.

FINDING A STYLE

A decorative style is about finding an overall theme for a room. It can be specific, such as country-inspired, or define a more general approach such as clean, fresh and uncluttered. Deciding on a style is the first step in planning decorative ideas. Think of it as the building block for your scheme which will help guide you through creative choices.

It's all too easy to get pulled off the decorative track by a sudden colour or pattern that catches your attention, so working to a specific style will help you decide if it will or won't work. Defining your style is also a way of ensuring that all the elements you do choose work together in harmony and create a complete and unified look. For example, if you decide on a modern theme of clean, simple lines you can immediately discount traditional floral patterns that would detract from the atmosphere you are hoping to create.

RESEARCHING A STYLE

If you have a specific style in mind, such as a historical decorative scheme, it's a good idea to find actual references and examples of rooms designed in this way. Perhaps you want to put back original features in a Victorian home, in which case borrow some books from your library and you can refer to these as you begin to put together your scheme.

Deciding on a style is a personal choice - you may find your notebook of ideas will help you here. But you will also need to consider the room itself, its atmosphere and ambience, and take into account practicalities such as size, shape and what the room is used for. You may fall in love with the idea of a grand, Regency-inspired scheme, but you need to ask yourself how it will translate within the proportions of the room you have in mind.

Once you have considered the basics and perhaps begun to formulate general ideas about your scheme you will now be ready to start making decisions. It is time to start thinking about choosing colour and pattern.

Above A daring combination of blue check patterns set against a neutral backdrop brings stunning originality to this living room.

PRACTICAL POINTERS

❖ Collect pictures showing colour combinations you like as a visual reference for ideas and schemes.

❖ Think about the amount of time you spend in a room, the way you use it and the kind of atmosphere that would be appropriate.

❖ The size and proportions of a room will influence the impact of any scheme. Consider ways to exploit or disguise these aspects through use of colour and pattern.

❖ Decide on an overall theme or style for your room. This will help you make the right design decision for the scheme you have in mind.

THE RIGHT SCHEME
FOR THE RIGHT ROOM

Every room has its own atmosphere which you may wish to exploit or disguise through decoration. You can make the most of a bright sunny room by choosing an equally vibrant and light colour scheme, while a dull plain room with few features can be brought to life when decked with pattern. If you've recently moved, spend a while sitting in the room to get a feel for the mood it radiates. Or if you're redecorating a room you know well, you might think about ways you can change its appearance. Consider the existing scheme too, looking at things that work well and aspects that are not so successful, and take these on board when planning the decor.

SIZE

The size of a room has a tremendous impact on any decorative scheme. Rich reds might look great in a spacious room, but in a tiny area could create a claustrophobic atmosphere. Also, remember that any pattern you choose should be the right scale for the proportions of the room. Large, voluminous patterns, for example, work well across smooth, uninterrupted areas of wall, and less imposing, regular designs are ideal for small rooms.

Colour and pattern are great deceivers of the eye and clever use of either can appear to reduce or increase the proportions of a room. A light coloured ceiling and vertical stripes on the wall give the illusion of added height; darker colours and more obvious patterns will tend to reduce the feeling of space.

Above *A minimalist style for one of the busiest rooms in the home means this kitchen will always be a joy to work in. One strong colour used throughout helps to retain an uncluttered atmosphere but gives a richness and impact to the pale walls and golden wood tones.*

FUNCTION

The way you use a room is an equally important factor when making choices about colour and pattern. In a hectic, busy kitchen, always full of people and clutter, a clean, simple scheme of light colours or a small pattern will detract from the visual chaos rather than add to it. Where a room is used as a place to unwind and relax, restful colours that are easy on the eye will probably be more suitable than bright dazzling decoration. An adventurous scheme can be a stunning change of mood to the rest of the home, but if you use the room a lot you need to consider whether you could live with it.

Decorative choices may also be determined by the amount of wear and tear a room endures. Paint might be more practical for an area used by children where accidental knocks can be simply and cheaply patched up.

EXISTING FURNISHINGS

Few people are lucky enough to start truly from scratch in a room and major purchases such as a carpet or suite of furniture invariably outlast several changes of decoration. It is essential to think about these when planning your scheme, but by looking for new ways to use colour and pattern to complement them you can still have a relatively free rein with creative solutions.

Soft furnishing fabrics could form the basis for a colour scheme. You may opt for darker or lighter shades, or choose to pick out a more subtle colour in the pattern as a link between the room and the wall decoration. Although flooring is an important part of any room, it may be neutral enough to work with a range of combinations. Accessories, too, can play a vital part in this situation. A rug or scatter of cushions that combine different colours used in the scheme will lend cohesion to the overall effect.

Above In a living room, a strong colour choice - such as this deep red - can evoke just the right mood for creating a cosy and relaxing atmosphere to retreat to. Relief patterned wallpaper has been used to embellish the walls giving softness and interest to the plain painted colour.

WORKING WITH COLOUR

Colour is the essence of any decorative scheme.
Whether plain or patterned, the choices we make about
colour have the greatest impact on the finished look of the room.
There is nothing quite so tantalising as the striking use of
colour, and nothing so inviting as warm, rich hues used to create
a cosy atmosphere. The brightest home can seem gloomy and
uninspiring beneath a cover of drab and dull tones. Conversely,
dark areas with little natural light can become radiant and airy
simply through the use of colour.

CHOOSING THE COLOURS

Many of us hanker after colourful interiors but lose confidence
when it comes to making final decisions. The main difficulty with
choosing colour is trying to imagine how it will look in the completed room. Then there is the task of selecting combinations of
complementary shades and considering how best to incorporate
them into a scheme.

The key to colour confidence, as with most aspects of decorating, is to give yourself plenty of time to think about and experiment with colours you would like to use. It is impossible to make
the right decision working from pattern books and paint charts
beneath artificial shop lighting. Ask for sample swatches and try
out your ideas in your room at home watching how different times
of day and your interior lighting affect their appearance.
Remember too, that choosing colour isn't an either/or situation:
don't feel obliged to choose either bold striking shades or fail-safe
standards such as white and cream. Successful colour scheming is
about finding combinations of tones and shades that complement
each other, and add interest and impact - and definition - to a
room. And that means understanding how each colour works.

COLOUR MOODS

You are probably aware that certain colours create certain moods
and atmospheres which can also extend to affecting the people
who use a room. Some colours project an aura of warmth; others
are cold and always appear more severe, and some shades, like
green, are naturally soothing to the eye and evoke a sense of calm.
Others, such as bright yellow, can be invigorating and cheerful to
be around. So, before deciding on a colour scheme, you should
decide on the atmosphere you hope to create. It would be a

Above *Dark colours don't need to
be sombre and can be the ideal
partner for touches of bright pattern
introduced as printed border
designs.*

Right *Fail-safe neutral colours are
easy to use with stronger colours.
Here a combination of white against
powder blue brings fresh vitality to
a small bathroom. White china
ornaments help to link the two decorative elements together.*

mistake to choose a cold colour like purple, for example, when you want to create a snug and cosy setting.

In general, the warm, cosy colours are deep reds, yellow ochres and rich greens. Bright yellows, soft greens and turquoise inject a sense of light and space into a room. Purples and bright blues can be cold and difficult to blend with other colours. That said, they can look stunning as a contrast to white and can evoke a fresh, simple look, ideal perhaps for a bathroom or guest bedroom. Increasingly popular, and for good reason, are washed-out tones of pale peaches, yellows and greens. As well as being gentle on the eye, so easy to live with, they provide a soft adaptable colour that can be both bright by day and inviting and welcoming by night.

PLAYING SAFE WITH COLOUR

White, off-white and creams are the sure-fire safe bets for any room. Whether a self-patterned wall covering or coat of paint, they provide a clean, fresh finish. They will work with any existing furnishings in the room and provide a simple backdrop to display pictures against. They can also be the perfect grounding for splashes of colour. Because they go with most shades you will discover that choosing a colour combination will be easy and fun. You can opt for deeper shades of cream or add a splash of bright shades to the woodwork. Toning shades will give a softer effect, contrasts will add accent and spark.

PRACTICAL POINTERS

❖ Successful schemes are not just about choosing colours that 'go' together. Any combination of shades must balance as well as complement one another.

❖ Too many strong colours in a room will jump out and be unsettling to spend time in.

❖ Try to choose one colour as your main theme and then look for other shades that can be used as an adjunct to this in smaller quantities for the finishing touches.

❖ If you're unsure about colour combinations, a golden rule is to choose different shades of the same colour; for example, a pale green on the wall edged with a stronger green.

WORKING WITH PATTERN

Pattern breathes life and rhythm into interiors, manipulating colour combinations as part of figurative or abstract shapes. It brings a sense of order through the repetition of design.

Pattern can become an intrinsic focal point of a scheme or through small regular designs can form nothing more than a background haze. Working with patterns can also make the job of choosing complementary colours for paintwork much more straightforward. Find a wallpaper you like and you have a ready-made palette of colours to choose from.

SETTING THE SCENE

Pattern brings its own mood to a room by the very token of the colours contained within it. Along with this, pattern is a very effective visual device for setting the scene. Certain patterns immediately conjure up specific atmospheres or styles of decoration and can therefore be a simple basis for a scheme you have in mind. For example, floral motifs set against the freshness of white instantly bring to mind country style. Darker tones of red and green set against cream or beige are reminiscent of traditional English interiors, while stripes offer classic simplicity. The scale of the pattern plays an equally important part; large sweeping designs suggest grandeur, small images of one colour give rustic overtones.

Pattern should be the right scale for the room and balance with the impact of furniture within it. If furniture is imposing, perhaps a simple pattern would be more effective. Patterns can be mixed successfully together, but finding a complementary balance is the trick to this. The best way to achieve a successfully coordinated room scheme is to take one pattern as the main theme, and then blend the other patterns and shades to work with it. You may also find that simple patterns in furnishing fabric will work well against regular patterned wallpaper.

Above Clever use of this large rambling pattern as a panel around a bedroom stops it from becoming too dominant. The plain painted area of wall matches the colour of the border and brings two very different treatments together as one cohesive look.

PAINT VERSUS WALLPAPER

Paint and wallpaper increasingly overlap when it comes to their decorative potential. Decorative finishes, once the domain of paint, are now available in printed pattern; whereas regular stripes, tiled effects and florals are now produced by the painter's brush. Most people have a natural inclination towards either smooth, flat painted walls, or feel happier with the texture of paper with so many printed options to choose from.

Time and practicalities, however, may be deciding factors in choosing between paint and wallpaper. For example, a paint effect wallpaper might be quicker to install than hours spent practising a similar effect with paint. However, it may be exactly that challenge that has prompted you to redecorate in the first place.

PRACTICAL POINTERS

❖ Choose colours that naturally appeal to you - you will find these easier to live with.

❖ Before you make your final choices, experiment with colour in a room, either as paint or pattern.

❖ Use pictures as inspiration and a guide for successful colour combinations.

❖ Think about the scale of a pattern, how large the repeat (the length of one complete pattern) is and whether this will overwhelm the room you have in mind.

❖ Balance the impact of different decorative elements. If you have chosen a strong, clear pattern, you should opt for a paint colour that will blend rather than add another competitive element.

CHOOSING PAINT

If colour is the essence of any decorative scheme, paint is one of the easiest, quickest and least expensive ways to introduce it. Paint is a vital decorating tool and a room is rarely completed without it being used in some way. It can be used on walls, woodwork, floors and furniture.

The veritable range of colours now available makes it possible for you to match almost exactly the colour you have in mind. Most large paint manufacturers offer a wide range of more subtle colours that are mixed to order to a set recipe.

Above *Using different types of paint together is the most immediate way to bring textural variety to areas of plain colour. Gloss and matt finishes are all that's needed to give this simple scheme of two colour tones a striking vibrancy.*

DECIDING ON WHAT YOU WANT

The beauty of paint is its versatility. It requires no skills to apply and only a few basic brushes. It can be used to sweep across whole walls, or for intricate detail work. And although the impressive appearance of decorative paint finishes might look like they need a professional's skilful eye, in fact, with a bit of practice they can be easily and cheaply achieved with just a few pots of paint.

Making choices about paint also means selecting the right type of finish for the impact and atmosphere you want to create as well as the job the paint must do. Deciding on the correct paint type means unravelling technical jargon and finding out what does what.

TYPES OF PAINT

Although there can seem a bewildering range of paint types to choose from, all those on the market fall into one of two categories: either oil-based or water-based. Oil-based paints tend to have a glossy sheen when dry and are soluble in white spirit; whereas water-based paints are only soluble in water and can be both glossy and matt when dry (see below).

Oil-based paints range from the traditional eggshell and gloss to durable sheen finishes and specialist lacquers or paints for metal. Water-based paints include emulsion, quick-drying eggshell and water-based gloss. In addition, some paints may have added ingredients such as vinyl, acrylic or polyurethane to make them more durable, or to increase their coverage.

WHAT'S WHAT

Liquid gloss Very shiny finish. Needs an undercoat and seal bare wood first with a primer. A combined primer and undercoat is available to save drying time. Mainly used for wood and metal, eg radiators. Coverage per litre: 17 sq m (20 sq yd).

Non-drip gloss High-shine finish. This paint has a gel-like texture and will not drip or run, nor does it require an undercoat. Mainly used for wood and metal, it is also good for plastic surfaces, eg guttering and drainpipes. Coverage per litre: 12 to 15 sq m (14 to 18 sq yd).

Self-undercoating gloss Combines the qualities of liquid and non-drip gloss. The paint has a thick, creamy consistency, it dries to a high-shine finish and covers most colours with a single coat. Used for wood, metal and plastic. Coverage per litre: 10 sq m (12 sq yd).

Mid-sheen oil-based paint Known commonly as eggshell. Harder wearing than emulsion paints, although not as tough as gloss varieties, this is a popular choice for woodwork where a less shiny finish is preferred. It does not need an undercoat but will usually require two or more coats. Can also be used on walls and metal. Coverage per litre: 16 sq m (19 sq yd).

Vinyl silk emulsion paint Silky, low-sheen finish. Does not need an undercoat and it is good for damp, steamy walls in kitchens and bathrooms. It can also be wiped clean. The silky finish emphasises flaws, however, especially if used on walls. But it is good for highlighting relief-pattern wall coverings. Used for walls and ceilings. Coverage per litre: 13 to 14 sq m (15 to 16 sq yd).

Vinyl matt emulsion paint Soft matt finish. This paint does not need an undercoat and it is the most common choice for walls and ceilings. Helps to disguise uneven surfaces. Coverage per litre: 14 to 15 sq m (16 to 18 sq yd).

Solid emulsion/roller paint Available in both matt and silk finishes, this paint does not need an undercoat. It also comes ready packed in a paint tray so it is easy to use. There is a limited number of colours available, however. They can be used on walls and ceilings. Thick texture will not drip or run. Coverage per litre: 12 sq m (14 sq yd).

Kitchen and bathroom paint Silky, low-sheen finish. Here is an emulsion paint with a high acrylic content making it more washable. It also contains a mild fungicide to guard again mould growth arising from condensation. Coverage per litre: 16 sq m (19 sq yd).

Undercoat As the name suggests, this is a first coat for certain types of paint to provide a surface for the top coat to adhere to. Check which undercoat the particular make or style of paint suggests.

Primer Bare wood (that has never been painted before) should be sealed with an appropriate primer. This seals the wood and creates a surface for paint.

NEWLY PLASTERED WALLS

If you are painting newly plastered walls you should leave them for at least four months to dry thoroughly before applying paint. Choose a water-based paint that will allow the surface to breathe. This will enable additional moisture in the walls to evaporate.

PRACTICAL POINTERS

❖ For the best effect, buy the same brand of primer, undercoat and gloss as they are designed to be used together.
❖ Solid emulsion paint is ideal for ceilings and stairwells as it doesn't drip. It is, however, more expensive than the more conventional emulsion paints.
❖ Oil-based paint is flammable, so store it outside the house, but protected from frost and damp.
❖ A small amount of lead exists naturally in undercoat, solvent-based primer and gloss paints, so if you want to avoid it, use water-based paints.

DECORATIVE PAINT EFFECTS

We often think of paint in terms of plain, flat colour. But the wonderful thing about using this material is its sheer versatility in creating texture and pattern. The simplest way to exploit the potential of paint in a room is to combine matt and gloss finishes. Most people do this without thinking when they decorate by using a shiny gloss paint for woodwork and a matt finish for the walls. Taking this one stage further, a coat of gloss paint on a panel of relief patterned wallcovering such as Anaglypta (see page 33) creates a striking contrast and decorative detail for plain painted walls.

SIMPLE PATTERNS

Another way to add a personal touch to decoration is by using paint to depict simple patterns such as checks or stripes. The slight unevenness of hand-crafted designs gives such finishes a unique charm and character all of their own. Paint applied using a sponging technique combines texture and pattern that can be muted or dazzling depending on the blends of colour you choose.

WHAT'S WHAT

Sponging and ragging

You probably recognise the soft paint textures known as sponging or ragging where, as the name suggests, a sponge or rag is used to apply a toning colour over a base coat to create a two-colour pattern. The impressive appearance of such treatments and the use of technical terms such as tinted glazes, has led to a certain mystique about these finishes and gives the impression that they are for the professional decorator only. But, in fact, such effects are deceptively simple and can be created using the most basic emulsion paint (see pages 40-1). Different shades of the same colour lends a gentle muted haze to walls that is

Left *You don't need to use special decorative techniques to have fun with paint. This sprinkling of pattern on a wall, for example, was painted freehand.*

Far Left *Paint as pattern can come straight from the tin, bold contrasts applied in different designs are an easy way to add colourful zest to a child's room.*

always easy to live with. More dramatic results come from using contrasts such as red over cream, or dark blue over green.

Colour washing
As the name suggests, colour washing uses an extremely diluted wash of colour that is applied on top of and designed to complement the base coat colour (see technique featured on pages 42-3).

Distressing
Newly painted furniture can look out of place in a room of traditional decoration but here is a finish that can transform the most modern piece with a disguise of well-worn age (see technique featured on page 44). Distressing is the most commonly used term where paint is rubbed down and certain colours added to make the piece appear to be older than it actually is.

Crackle glaze
This paint effect looks rather like peeling paint. Contrasting colours for the base and top coats suggest many layers of paint and can

Above *The art of distressing lends a patina of age to newly painted walls. Using closely toning colours sourced from a furnishing fabric helps unify different decorative elements of the room.*

Left *A marbled paint effect can be utilised for the fluid haze of pattern it lends to walls. Here, the marbling provides a perfect balance to the cluttered style of this small bathroom.*

instantly make the piece or area of woodwork look considerably older (see technique featured on page 45).

Marbling
This paint effect is suitable for period interiors and works well in panels or on furniture. Although slightly more ambitious than the techniques mentioned above, nonetheless marbling is also readily achievable (see technique featured on pages 46-7).

Stencils A stencil is a cut-out design template through which colour is applied. The motif can be used in repeat to create a border or an all-over impression of pattern on walls, or it can be used as a way of creating a larger, single image that works as a feature in its own right. Pattern applied through stencilling has a faded patina that blends well with the background paint colour (see technique featured on pages 48-9).

Trompe l'oeil The grandest decorative illusion is the visual trickery known as trompe l'oeil where paint is used to create a three-dimensional image, such as a fireplace or a tendril of ivy winding across a corner of a room. Although traditionally used to portray intricate scenes across a whole wall, the technique of trompe l'oeil can be used on a small scale to startling effect, such as a rug or book incorporated into a painted floor.

Left *Colour washed walls provide a softly textured setting for the faded charm of stencilled motifs. The design look ambitiously complicated but it is, in fact, made up from a number of pre-cut stencils and can be simply executed using ordinary emulsion paint.*

PAINTED DETAILS

The success of any room scheme depends on how all
the elements are brought together to form a cohesive look.
An effective way to link the different colour elements, such as
patterned wallcovering with curtains or furniture, pale painted
walls with patterned furnishings, is by introducing
complementary shades in the form of paint details. Vibrant
colours provide a sparkle of lively accent, deeper toning
shades complete a relaxing and restful scheme.

WOODWORK

Skirting boards, doors and window frames add definition to any
scheme. Woodwork can be left as a natural wood finish or, more
commonly, painted. Traditionally, woodwork is painted in a
white gloss finish which simplifies a scheme. But colour is a more
exciting option. Pick a shade from a wallpaper that complements
furnishings or flooring in the room. If walls are pale and plain a
slightly deeper or brighter choice provides a neat finishing edge.

Complete contrasts of colour can be striking, but beware of
shades that might overpower. Splashes of red against cream walls
in a kitchen will balance the impact of wooden units, deep blue
woodwork in a mainly white bathroom lends freshness and
sophistication. But in a living room of plain, pale tones a sudden
shock of deep green or rust may jar against the pervading softness
of the atmosphere.

Above An ordinary shelf unit is turned into a decorative feature with a lick of
strident colour. It helps to break up the otherwise nondescript appearance of
white painted tongue and groove panelling.

WALLS

Picture rails, positioned towards the top of walls, and dado rails, positioned about a third of the way up, can be a key place to introduce colour. It can add order to patterned walls and help to break up large expanses of plain coloured surfaces. For simplicity, use the same colour as for other woodwork in the room. But where everything is neutral, a dado rail or picture rail can be just the place to add a spark of something stronger or brighter without going over the top and upsetting the balance of the scheme.

FURNITURE

Painted furniture can be one of the best ways to bring wall colour into the room and take colour from furnishings back to the wall. It can also be a useful device for refocusing the balance of colour. For example, if walls are rather over-powering, you could use colours from soft furnishings on a piece of furniture near the wall to help give these more emphasis. The wallspace itself can be given added impact by decorating shelving with colours that match the woodwork or soft furnishings.

Left Painted details are a useful device to link different areas and tones of a room. By introducing the bright yellow of the windows onto the dado rail, the sharply contrasting colours used in this room fit together as one complete scheme.

CHOOSING WALLPAPERS

In one sense, choosing a wallpaper poses less difficulties than choosing paints. Most of us know what we like when we see it, be it a colour combination or particular motif that instantly appeals. And with the plethora of designs to choose from there are styles to suit everyone's taste. It is best to choose wallpaper before paint since it is easier to match a shade of paint to a pattern than the other way round.

Above There are no rules to say you can't mix patterns, but it's important to consider how different scales of design will work together. Decide which area of pattern is your focal point - walls, curtains or furnishings - and pick less imposing designs to complement rather than compete with this.

ASSESSING THE DESIGN

As with any other decorative choices, a small sample swatch can be deceptive and colours that seem subtle in a pattern book can suddenly become strong and overwhelming when used throughout a room. The golden rule is try a pattern at home in a room before making final decisions. The larger the sample, the better idea you will get of the overall effect. Some shops may allow you to take a roll home of a pattern you like. If this is not possible, ask whether you can order a larger sample swatch.

The key thing to look at in any wallpaper design is the size of the pattern. Then you need to weigh up whether the scale is appropriate for the height and length of the walls in the room it will be used. You also need to think about the colour of the main element in the design. On a small sample, a strong green may balance well with the reds and blues around it, but when used on a large area this might become much more dominant. Likewise, a small pattern that looks fresh and colourful might get lost on large expanses of wall, paling to insignificance.

It is also important to remember the overall atmosphere you are trying to create and to look at how the pattern you like will influence this. Regular designs, for example, invariably add a sense of formality.

Practicalities may also have a say in the patterns you choose. If this is your first attempt at wallpapering you may prefer to avoid complicated figures that require accurate matching, and go for an all-over pattern or a mottled paint-effect finish that may be easier to work with. If your walls are rather uneven with irregular corners, a clean, simple stripe may look odd and highlight these aspects, while a small floral covering would work well as a foil for such imperfections.

There is, of course, a wide range of textured wallcoverings that can be used as an excellent base for painted colour and for adding decorative detail to walls. And when it comes to adding finishing touches, printed coverings and borders can be used in a variety of ways to finish off wallpapered areas and introduce pattern into a plain scheme

WHAT'S WHAT

Available in myriad patterns, there are many different types of wallpaper to choose from. Although an ordinary wallpaper is often the option for printed designs, in rooms where practical considerations are as important as appearance, such as in a kitchen or child's bedroom, you may prefer to make your choice from a range of washable coverings.

Lining paper Professionals invariably line walls with lining paper as a base for decorative paper, but this is not essential. Where the surface of the wall is poor and uneven, however, lining paper is advisable since it provides a smoother base. Always use the same strength of paste for the lining paper and the wallpaper. Lining paper can also be used as a base for flat paint as it gives a softer appearance to plastered walls.

Woodchip Used as a textured base for paint, this paper has pieces of wood embedded into it giving an all-over random effect. It is good for disguising damaged or uneven walls. Water-based matt emulsion and flat oil-based eggshell paint are the best options for this paper.

Relief wallcoverings
These have an embossed pattern which can be used as a decorative feature on walls and are often available with coordinating borders. Shiny paint finishes, such as vinyl silk emulsion, will highlight the pattern, whereas matt emulsion or eggshell will subdue it. More heavily embossed papers, designed to imitate plasterwork, and commonly known as Anaglypta, can be used as all-over coverings or for dado panels and borders.

Ordinary wallpaper
Printed, plain or patterned. Usually spongeable but rarely washable so may be unsuitable for heavy-wear areas.

Washable or vinyl-coated wallpaper A printed paper with a thin vinyl coating which can be cleaned with a cloth and soapy water. Quite hard-wearing so good for kitchens and kids' rooms. When applying borders on top of such papers you will need to use a special adhesive; check with your supplier.

Paper-backed vinyl
Plastic film on a paper backing sheet which is available printed and sometimes with an embossed pattern. This type of wallpaper can be cleaned with a mild abrasive and is ideal for kitchens and bathrooms. If applying a border you will need to use a special adhesive; check with your supplier.

Foamed vinyl Paper backing with a top surface of PVC. Usually imitates tiling. Also water-resistant, so it is a good alternative to ceramic tiles for kitchens and bathrooms.

'Special' wallcoverings
All papers with textile or natural-look finishes such as silk, hessian or cork. Often very expensive and may require special hanging methods and adhesive. They also require special treatment to remove them from the walls when re-decorating.

FLORAL DESIGNS

Inspired by nature, floral wallpapers have an inherent warmth and familiarity which is easy to live with. They also provide a good source of colour combinations to incorporate with your scheme. Set against a white background they can be refreshing and lively, while richer blends and all-over hazes of colour are at once cosy and inviting. Soft peachy tones are ideal for bedrooms, and reds, browns and rusts create the perfect setting for living rooms.

The scale of patterns varies immensely. Too large or too strong a design can be overwhelming against pale colours or when used in a small space. But florals work well with the simplicity of stripes and checks, the informality of one offsetting the formality of the latter.

If you're using obvious floral patterns on the walls it is advisable to keep the rest of the room simple: stripes or checks in toning colours provide a good balance. Many companies now produce coordinating fabrics designed to complement wallpapers, and these are worth considering if you want to blend patterns.

Left, above and right *Florals provide a versatile theme for patterned wallcoverings and there is bound to be one to suit the atmosphere and mood you want to create, be it country-cottage freshness, traditional Victorian style or the romantic allure of watercolour pastels.*

SMALL PATTERNS

In most homes where rooms are simply not large enough for sweeping grand designs, it is often better to go for a small pattern on the walls and introduce larger motifs on curtains or in furnishing fabrics. Whether floral, figurative or geometric, small prints that relate to the overall scheme or style of a room add colour and interest to walls, without conflicting with pattern used elsewhere in the room. They are equally successful as the backdrop for plain schemes.

If the design loses some of its impact when incorporated into the rest of the scheme, select a strong colour from the pattern to use on the woodwork. This will help to redress the balance.

Above For this pretty pink living room, a small patterned paper provides the perfect backdrop to the more-eyecatching furnishing fabric. By choosing the same blends of colour the two work together harmoniously without competing for attention.

STRIPES

Timeless, classic, contemporary or traditional, striped wallcoverings are one of the most successful decorative options. Stripes bring colour to a wall-space most effectively, but they are simple and elegant enough to work against almost any pattern. That said, stripes come in a wide range of designs and widths and it is important to choose an appropriate one for the size of the room. Slightly wider stripes are better across a large area, fine stripes work well in small rooms.

Striped wallcoverings can also give the illusion of height since they draw the eye upwards, and for low ceilings this can be ideal. If walls already seem to tower above you, choose a wider stripe (this draws the eye across rather than up) and consider adding dado or picture rails (if they are not already in place) to break up the vertical lines.

PAINT EFFECT WALLPAPERS

When paint effect finishes such as sponging and ragging entered the decorator's vocabulary in the early 1980s, so wallpaper manufacturers spotted a gap in the market. It is hard to tell these soft, muted papers from the real thing, and they really are the answer if you want textured colour but don't have the time or inclination to apply it yourself.

These papers are a versatile option that blend well in a variety of situations and colour schemes. They are available in a wide range of colours from rich reds and blues to dreamy peaches and greens.

Above *Paint effect wallpapers are a great way to add textured colour to walls. Here, a rag-rolled pattern in watery green is used to divide up large expanses of wall in a hallway. A delicate floral border picks up the colour and style of both papers.*

Right *Stripes are one of the most versatile of patterns. If striped walls look too uniform for comfort, why not add a complementary border? Choose a similar colour scheme with a thread of contrasting colour for a striking accent.*

TRADITIONAL STYLE

Traditional style interiors are as popular today as they have ever been. Wallpaper manufacturers offer a range of papers to reflect these tastes, varying from those inspired by classic designs, but updated in modern colours, to accurate reproductions of authentic period pattern.

If you are reinstating original features in a Victorian house, a William Morris style paper evoking the arts and crafts period of the later nineteenth century may help to set the scene for what you are trying to create. It is, however, important to remember that decorative tastes were different in the past. Patterns were strong and the tendency was towards a cluttered effect. This might be too imposing in a family house of the 1990s and you may need to temper inspiration with the practicalities of the way you live today. One way is to take authentic papers and blend these with a more vivacious, contemporary colour scheme.

RELIEF-PATTERN PAPERS

One inspiration of the past that works well in a variety of styles is the traditional self-patterned relief papers, such as Anaglypta wallcoverings. Look at any Victorian interior and you will see this used in abundance. The papers are designed to be painted and come in a selection of weights, from those suitable for use as wallcoverings to thicker decorative panelled detail that traditionally ran beneath the dado rail in hallways.

These wallcoverings can be especially effective when painted in silk emulsions or gloss paints which highlight the pattern of the paper. Use contrasting shades or complementary tones to create a striking division of the wallspace. Choose from small to grand sweeping designs, set against coordinating friezes or borders.

Above One way to put back the style of a period home is to opt for patterns of the past like this Arts and Crafts paper.

Left If you want to give plain colour schemes a little more decorative verve, relief patterned wallpapers, designed to be painted, could be the answer.

THE FINISHING TOUCH

As well as being an attractive way for covering walls, printed papers and borders can be used to give a clean, finishing edge to wallspace, create decorative effects and, indeed, introduce pattern to plain areas.

BORDERS

Wallpaper borders are now frequently a part of the whole room setting and most wallcoverings offer a wide selection of coordinating designs. Their primary purpose is to provide clean lines at the edge of a patterned (or plain) section, such as the top of walls or at the base along skirting boards and around door frames. Positioned in place of or adjacent to picture rails and dado rails they help to give wall space a natural sense of division and proportion. Narrow, simply designed borders can also be used to create decorative panels on plain, painted walls.

Printed patterns can also be transformed into original and highly imaginative treatments in the form of découpage finishes. Sections of pattern can be cut out (specially produced pre-cut motifs are also available) and applied to walls. With a selection of black and white motifs from original framed prints you could, for example, set about creating your own version of a traditional Victorian print room.

Above Available in a wealth of colours, patterns and styles, wallpaper borders offer all sorts of creative potential for any scheme or room.

Left A floral cut-out motif sets an uninspiring corner blossoming with colour.

Far left Transform plain painted walls by using lengths of wallpaper border to create decorative panels. You can make more of this idea by running them around pictures or wall ornamentation.

USING PAINTS AND WALLPAPERS

Creative decorating choices don't need to end with decisions about which wallpaper or which paint colour. These basic ingredients can be put to work to create all manner of wonderful visual effects simply by using different techniques and methods to apply them. If you covet a completely individual and original look for your home, getting to grips with one or two of these ideas will prove immensely satisfying, exciting to do, and amply repay the extra time and effort invested in them. A decorative paint finish such as sponging or ragging, for example, turns an ordinary pot of paint into a source of rich texture and pattern; or a wallpaper border can become a feature in itself when cut and shaped into a panel detail on painted walls.

Of course, even the most stunning visual creation must be appropriate for the room, atmosphere and scheme you have in mind. Each treatment brings its own personality and influence to the rest of the room, so you will need to consider how such ideas might be incorporated as part of the scheme. If a striking, all-over effect is not for you, perhaps the discreet charm of a stencilled motif would be a more suitable finishing touch.

Discovering the potential for using paint and wallpaper is an adventure in itself. And once you begin to explore this way of working you will find a wealth of possibilities for adding original flair and charm to your home. But while you may be itching to get on and do the real thing it's always worth setting time aside for practice and experimentation, trying different techniques as well as colour combinations. This will give you a clear picture of how the finished effect will look - it might even spark some ideas of your own.

Right Painted stripes above wood panelling of the same colour show how simple effects can create stunning visual decoration.

DECORATIVE PAINT EFFECTS:
Practice makes perfect
Paint effect know-how

SPONGING AND RAGGING:
What to do
Variations on a theme
Bright ideas
Variations on a theme

COLOUR WASHING:
What to do
Bright ideas

DISTRESSING:
What to do
Bright ideas

CRACKLE GLAZE:
What to do

MARBLING:
What to do
Practical pointers

STENCILLING:
What to do
Bright ideas
Practical pointers

STRIPES AND CHECKS:
What to do
Bright ideas
Practical pointers

PAINTED FURNITURE
What to do
Bright ideas

PAINTED FLOORS:
Preparing wood floors
What to do
Bright ideas

PAINTING TEXTURED WALL-COVERINGS:
Bright ideas
Practical pointers

WALLPAPER BORDERS:
Position of borders
Bright ideas
Practical pointers

DECOUPAGE:
What to do
Bright ideas

DECORATIVE PAINT EFFECTS

If you're fed up with plain painted walls, but don't want to wallpaper, decorative paint effects could be the answer. A simple pot of emulsion paint contains the potential for all manner of sumptuous visual effects. As well as hiding a multitude of sins in a room, such as uneven wall surfaces or irregular walls, they are hard to equal when it comes to adding zest and originality to a room. All you have to add is a bit of time and creative courage.

Most decorative treatments, such as sponging or ragging, involve applying one or two broken layers of coloured paint over a neutral or contrasting base colour. In this way, the two colours can be seen together in the form of a textured pattern. The way in which the 'coloured' layers are applied, or treated while wet, dictates the appearance of the final finish. The colours you choose are also an important factor. Subtle tones produce a soft haze of texture that works well as a background to any scheme, while contrasting colours make a more dynamic statement and could become a feature in themselves.

PRACTICE MAKES PERFECT

An undeserved mystique surrounds the art of decorative paint effects and confusing and baffling terms give the impression that they are for the professional decorator's palette alone. In fact, they are relatively easy to get to grips with. There is, of course, no substitute for practice and experimentation before attempting the real thing and lining paper is ideal for this.

Having a go at the treatment will give you a feel for the techniques required, how much paint to use, how quickly to work - even handling a paint-covered sponge can be tricky at first - and will give you more confidence when it comes to the real thing. You may even decide to swap your sponge for a rag-rolled finish!

Above A sumptuous textural finish was created for the walls in this living room by rag-rolling red over a cream base-coat.

water-based. However, since either can be used for most of the ideas given here, instructions refer to coloured glazes only. But you can use any of the following mediums.

Water-based glaze

Emulsion paint can be used to create most decorative finishes and is the easiest to work with. For the best results, dilute the paint with water before use: one part paint to three parts water. You can vary this slightly, depending on the strength of colour you want to use. Add a few drops of glycerine if you find the paint dries too quickly when working. Water-based glazes can only be used on walls painted with matt emulsion.

Thinned oil paint glaze

Alternatively, you could use flat, oil-based paint. Dilute it with white spirit: one part paint to three parts white spirit. The resulting glaze can be used on walls and woodwork over base coats of emulsion or eggshell.

Scumble glaze

Professional decorators use a tinted, transparent oil-based glaze, known as a scumble glaze, for paint effect treatments because of its translucent quality. Because it dries so slowly, if you make a mistake you can always wipe the glaze off and start again. Transparent oil-based glazes are available from paint suppliers and specialist shops in matt, mid-sheen or gloss. The glaze should be thinnned with white spirit and can then be tinted with eggshell paint or artist's oil colour, also available from art shops. A typical 'recipe' is one part eggshell paint, two parts of transparent glaze, with two to three parts of white spirit.

PAINT EFFECT KNOW-HOW

The base coat Paint effects are worked by applying one or two colours (glazes) over a plain painted base coat. The base coat should be of either water-based emulsion paint or flat oil-based paint, known as eggshell. It should be dry (if recently painted), clean and grease-free.

Glazes You can use emulsion paint straight from the tin to create textured paint effects, but you may find the finish is rather heavy and obvious. More commonly, colours are specially prepared to produce a finer, more translucent textured pattern. These are called glazes if they are oil-based and washes if

SPONGING AND RAGGING

Sponging and ragging are the easiest and most adaptable of the textured paint effects. One or two colours are applied with a sponge or rag to produce a cohesive, all-over pattern. In toning colours the finish will be subtle and muted, in contrasting shades more obvious. These effects can be used on walls, woodwork, doors and fireplaces, as well as on smaller objects such as furniture - even vases. They are also useful for camouflaging unsightly features such as radiators and pipes.

If you are sponging, make sure that you use a natural marine sponge, as the irregular surface and soft texture give the best results. Man-made sponges can be used, but they will create a more uniform and less interesting effect. For ragging, any cloth will do. The crisper the fabric, the more defined the pattern, while soft cloths with a close weave lend a subtle, evocative look. The action of the rag, dabbing or rolling, also affects the final result.

WHAT TO DO - SPONGING

1 Make sure the base coat is dry, clean and grease-free.

2 Pour the glaze into the roller tray.

3 Wet the sponge thoroughly with water and then squeeze all the water out until it is almost dry. The sponge will then return to its original size.

YOU WILL NEED

Prepared quantity of glaze (see page 39)

Paint roller tray

Natural marine sponge or 3m (3yd) of rags

Short length of lining paper

4 Dip the flattest side of the sponge into the glaze, removing any excess on the side or ridged part of the tray, and then dab it on a piece of lining paper. This will help distribute the glaze evenly over the sponge and guards against any blobs in the final pattern. The print should show a distinct texture: if the texture blurs, the sponge is too wet.

5 To apply the glaze, stand at arm's length and dab the sponge very gently onto the wall. Use a slight rolling motion each time you dab, and change direction every time you lift the sponge to create an even, mottled effect. The less pressure you apply, the more delicate the final pattern.

6 Aim to cover the ground coat completely with sponged 'prints' while still allowing the colour from the base to show through. Take up more glaze whenever the pattern begins to look faint, remembering to dab off any excess before going back to the wall each time. Work quickly and evenly and complete one whole area of wall at one time to keep colour and texture even.

7 Wring the sponge out from time to time to prevent a build-up of colour obscuring its surface texture. If the sponge becomes clogged with glaze, rinse under warm water (or in white spirit for oil-based glazes), and squeeze dry again before continuing with the next area of wall.

Above *Sponging techniques are the simplest way to apply texture to surfaces. Always experiment with different colour combinations and strength of colour before working on the real thing.*

BRIGHT IDEAS

❖ By changing the shape of the fabric or the way you use it to apply the glaze you can create a variety of different effects. Roll the fabric into a fat sausage shape and with a hand at either end roll the fabric in a downwards action. Overlap sections, change directions and the amount of pressure.

❖ For a richer effect you could apply a second layer of colour. If you decide to do this, make the first coat fairly sparse and overlap the second colour to give an even finish. Use a different sponge or clean piece of rag for each colour. Leave the first colour to dry overnight before applying the second.

❖ Use the same actions to remove colour and create a negative version of the textured effect - this is known as sponging or ragging off. Oil-based glazes are best for this since emulsion glazes dry so quickly. Paint a strip of eggshell paint or glaze over the base coat about 1m (1yd) wide and while it is still wet work a sponging action into the surface taking off some of the top colour to create a textured pattern. The more frequently you sponge over the area, the less distinct the pattern will become. Complete one wall at a time before it dries.

WHAT TO DO - RAGGING

1 Prepare the paint as for sponging, above.

2 Cut a piece of rag large enough to form a loosely crumpled pad about the size of your hand. (The size of fabric you need will depend on how thick it is; cut subsequent pieces to the same size.) Check that the side you will use to apply paint has interesting bunches and folds since this will form the pattern.

3 Dip the bunched cloth in the glaze and blot any excess on a piece of lining paper. Do a test print: it should be clear and obvious, if it blurs, the fabric is too wet.

4 Ragging is best done as a rhythmic, systematic dabbing action. Overlap prints and dab in different directions to ensure an even but irregular pattern. The texture can be varied by rearranging the cloth at regular intervals and varying the amount of pressure you use to apply the paint.

5 If the pattern begins to fade, take up more glaze. Change the cloth when it becomes sodden with glaze and unworkable - the pattern will become softer and less clear when this happens. Complete one area of wall at a time to ensure an even finish.

VARIATIONS ON A THEME

Dragging Use a bristled brush, dragged through glaze applied to the wall to create fine stripes. Work 1m (1yd) wide strips at a time.

Spattering This effect imitates the textured surface of granite or stone. Load your brush with diluted emulsion paint, taking care to wipe the excess off against a hard rim. Then gently run your finger across the bristles to release a fine spray of paint droplets.

Stippling This provides a gently mottled effect ideal as a background haze of colour on walls. Paint glaze onto a painted surface working 1m (1yd) wide strips at a time. With a stippling brush, press into the wet glaze to break up the surface (a bit like sponging). Clean the brush frequently since it is liable to become clogged with glaze.

COLOUR WASHING

Colour washes are the light touch of decorating. As the name suggests, this technique uses an extremely diluted wash of colour which is applied on top of and as an adjunct to, a base coat colour. They lend a lively radiance to walls in any room and can be a useful finishing trick to shift the balance and impact of colours.

Because the paint is so dilute, strong shades can be used without any fear that they will dominate. A rich red wash, for example, will add warmth to a yellow base, while a wash of bright yellow will add a luminous clarity to a yellow base. A white wash can be an effective way to fade or tone down colours that are too strong and, by the same token, colours that have turned out to be not quite how you imagined can be transformed by adding a pale coat of a complementary colour. They are simple and easy to apply, and you can use a number of layers of the same or different shades to build up the finished look you want.

YOU WILL NEED

Water-based emulsion paint

Medium-sized container

Wide paintbrush with soft bristles

Above The look you create with paint effects is a personal choice; you may, for example, decide to use a less diluted colour wash to achieve a stronger blend of colour tones.

WHAT TO DO

1 Make sure the walls are dry, clean and grease-free.

2 Dilute the emulsion paint in the container, mixing one part paint to nine parts water.

3 A colour wash is very thin and watery and liable to create drips and water marks. To minimise this, work swiftly and quickly with sweeping and vigorous brush strokes. Try not to linger on one spot too long otherwise you may begin to dissolve the underlying colour. The wash dries very quickly, so brush marks are inevitable. A few drops of glycerine in the paint will slow down the drying time.

4 The wash will be dry and ready for another coat in half an hour. You may find you have to do up to four or five coats of wash to create the desired depth of colour and impact you want.

BRIGHT IDEAS

❖ Use the same colour as the base coat to give a hint of texture to painted walls.

❖ Stronger toning shades will add vibrant brilliance to the base coat colour, rich reds can add warmth, pale colours will fade the base colour.

❖ Unhappy with the colour of paint you've chosen, or perhaps the walls seem distant from the rest of the room? Use a wash to shift the tonal balance, matching the shade to that used in furniture or curtains to help link the elements together.

❖ Use several coats of a wash to build up the strength of colour and effect you want.

❖ Use broad sweeping strokes to avoid drips and water marks. Don't work on one area for too long at a time since this will begin to dissolve the underlying colour.

Right Fail safe cream comes to life with a wash of sunshine yellow. Apply several coats, building up the intensity of colour until you achieve the look you want.

DISTRESSING

Newly painted woodwork or furniture can sometimes seem too neat and new for a traditional scheme. One way round this is to distress the surface, which means using paint to give it a sense of age and wear. There are a number of simple ways to create this effect and you could experiment with a combination of ideas. Toning colours mixed with one stronger shade will give vibrancy to the finish, for example. Distressing is especially effective for areas with relief pattern such as skirting, doors, dado and picture rails, tongue and groove wood panelling and relief patterned wallpapers.

YOU WILL NEED

Small quantities of 2 or 3 different coloured glazes (see page 39)

Ten 30 x 30cm (12 x 12in) squares of lint-free rag

White spirit (for oil-based glazes only)

Small paintbrush

Narrow paintbrush

Polyurethane varnish

BRIGHT IDEAS

❖ For a truly well-worn effect, apply two or three shades of colour, starting with the palest as the base coat. When dry, rub the surface with sandpaper to allow random streaks of colour to show.

❖ To mellow the finished effect, tint the polyurethane with artist's oil colour in burnt umber.

WHAT TO DO

1 Choose glazes that match and tone with the colour of the base coat.

2 Check that area to be distressed is dry, clean and grease-free.

3 Moisten one piece of rag. If you are using oil-based glazes use white spirit, if you are using a water-based glaze use water.

4 Apply the first colour of glaze quickly, using the narrow paintbrush to work the glaze into the recesses of the surface you are decorating. Work on an area 2m (2yd) long or square at a time.

5 Use the moistened rag to remove the glaze from raised parts of the surface leaving only the recesses with added colour. Continue all the way over the surface you are distressing. Leave to dry.

6 For a graded and more obvious effect, repeat the process using a darker shade of glaze.

7 Seal the treatment with polyurethane varnish.

CRACKLE GLAZE

A crackle glaze creates a cracked and broken surface, rather like old, peeling paint. The beauty and versatility of this finish is the way the base coat is allowed to shine through between the cracks of the top layer. The effect works best on furniture, and crackle glaze is available from art shops.

YOU WILL NEED

2 colours of water-based emulsion paints

Crackle glaze

Paintbrush

Oil-based varnish

WHAT TO DO

1 Prepare the surface of the piece of furniture to be painted (see page 53).

2 Apply the base colour paint and leave it to dry.

3 Brush the crackle glaze over the base colour paint. Try to keep the brush strokes running in the same direction, either all horizontally or vertically. Allow the glaze to dry for about an hour in a warm, well-ventilated room. The glaze works best when painted on flat, horizontal surfaces so, where possible, lie pieces of furniture on their sides.

4 Working quickly from one side to the other apply the top coat of paint colour, being sure to apply the paint evenly over the whole surface. The glaze reacts with this top coat very quickly so do not attempt to paint over the surface since it will already have started to crack.

5 When completely dry, seal with an oil-based varnish (the crackle glaze reacts with an acrylic varnish).

Left Tongue and groove panelling is the perfect place to set distressed paint effects to work - here, contrasting streaks of colour punctuate shades of soft green.

MARBLING

Marbling has been used for centuries where the natural material was either too scarce or too expensive to use. It is one of the most impressive paint finishes with its fine threads of coloured veins running haphazardly across the surface. Although it looks complicated, in fact the effect is drawn by using layers of different paint effect techniques which together conjure up a most eye-catching illusion.

Find a picture of a marble which you like to use as a guide - you don't have to stick to the same colours but could use the general colour scheme of a room as the inspiration instead. In general, close tones of the same colour, with a contrasting shade for veins, are the easiest route to a successful result and it's probably best to stick to these if this is your first time at marbling. A light touch combined with confident strokes are the secret to achieving a good finish so practice is crucial.

Marbling works best on small areas in places where the material might originally have been used, such as furniture, fireplaces or areas of wood panelling.

To marble, use different layers of glaze while it is still wet. For this, oil-based glazes (see page 39) are best since they take longer to dry and give a more translucent quality. They should be darker than the base coat.

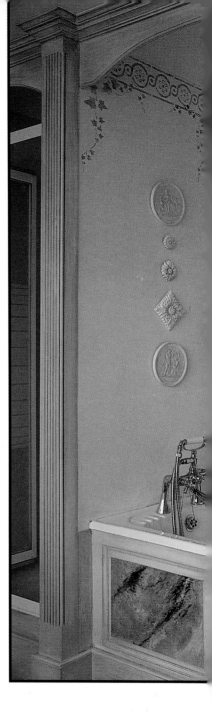

YOU WILL NEED

Medium-sized paintbrush

2 or 3 toning colours of glaze (see page 39)

2 darker coloured glazes for veining

Clean, lint-free rags

Medium-sized artist's paint-brush

Fine-sized artist's paint-brush

Feather or dry, soft paint-brush

Polyurethane varnish

WHAT TO DO

1 Check that your base coat is dry, clean and grease-free.

2 With the medium-sized paintbrush, paint the base coat with the palest coloured glaze (it should be slightly darker than your base coat).

3 Roll up a dry piece of rag into a fat sausage shape, long enough for you to roll with both hands. While the glaze is still wet, roll the rag across the painted surface to lift off patches of glaze (see ragging off on page 41) and create a textured pattern. Aim to expose between one-half and two-thirds of the base colour. Complete the whole area to be marbled in this way.

4 To achieve the characteristic translucency and depth of marble, repeat the process using a further two layers of slightly darker glaze. (Apply as many layers of toning glaze as you like to achieve the appearance you wish, but three should be adequate.)

Left *You may not be able to afford the luxury of real marble, but you can have a go at imitating the wonderful translucent patterns of this material by employing a combination of paint effect treatments.*

5 Using the medium-sized artist's paintbrush and a darker glaze, paint on irregular patches about 5cm wide to suggest the areas of compression. While the patches are still wet, use a rag to lift and smudge the glaze until it blends with the background colours already applied. Soften the effect further by rubbing a dry brush lightly across the area.

6 To create the veins, apply a dark or contrasting coloured glaze with the fine-sized artist's paintbrush. Work the veins in the darker patches and try to vary the thickness and direction to create the natural random appearance of marble. While the glaze is still wet, lightly smudge the lines using the feather or dry soft paintbrush.

7 Leave to dry and then seal with a coat of polyurethane varnish.

STENCILLING

When it comes to using paint as pattern, there is nothing to match the charm of hand-painted stencil motifs. Stencils were used primarily as a way to speed up repetitive decoration. They were particularly popular in eighteenth-century America when wallpaper was in short supply, and it is these simple faded images that have become synonymous with stencilling finishes today. However, there is nothing to say that stencils can't be bright, bold and contrasting and in this way they can be especially good for brightening up a child's bedroom, kitchen or bathroom.

Ordinary emulsion paint and a stubby, flat-ended stencil brush are all you need to paint a stencilled motif. Mix the emulsion paint with a little water to a creamy consistency, so that it is thin enough not to clog the brush but not so thin that the paint will run when applied.

YOU WILL NEED

Spirit level

Coloured blackboard chalk

Stencil (pre-cut or cut by yourself)

Masking tape

Emulsion paints

Flat-ended stencil brush

Piece of lining paper

WHAT TO DO

1 Use the spirit level to mark a horizontal guide-line across each wall for positioning the stencil. Use coloured blackboard chalk which will wipe off easily when you have finished.

2 Matching the horizontal line on your stencil to the chalk guideline on the wall, fix the stencil in place using small strips of masking tape. A small design can be worked from one corner of a wall to the next, for a larger motif it might be better to start in the centre of each wall and work outwards to the left- and right-hand corners in turn.

3 Dip the stencil brush into the paint, you will need hardly any. Blot the brush onto the lining paper until it is nearly dry.

Right A colour wash paint finish makes the perfect backdrop for the faded patina of traditional-style stencilled motifs.

Left *Closely toning shades of colour lend a delicate ambience to a stencilled border made up from a selection of different style shells.*

4 Using small circular brush strokes, dab the brush over the stencil working outwards from the centre. Don't feel you have to create a solid block of colour, and try to vary the intensity of the paint, working more into some areas to give a shaded effect. For more depth in simple motifs, work tiny areas of a contrasting or darker toning colour over the same stencil. Use a different stencil brush and work while the first colour is still wet to blend the two together.

5 Remove the stencil from the wall. Wipe clean with a dry paper towel or rag taking care to remove paint from the edges. Then reposition the stencil using your guidelines to show you where the next motif should be. Fix in place as before and repeat the stencilling process.

6 If you are using more than one stencil and colour for a motif, wait for the first colour to dry before working the next one.

STRIPES AND CHECKS

With just a few small brush strokes, a stunning ensemble of lines and shapes can be conjured up, ranging from classic stripes to harlequin checks - even a tiling effect. Although painting such designs might seem an unnecessary effort given the wide range of similarly patterned wallpapers to choose from, the personal touch that comes with these hand-painted images cannot be matched in print. Also, of course, colour, size and style of the design can be tailor-made for your scheme. All you need is a few simple tools - a paintbrush, or roller - a relatively steady hand and some patience to draw up the design.

BRIGHT IDEAS

❖ Give simple stripes a textured appearance by using a paint roller. Tie string around the roller to make two raised sections which create the striped effect. To ensure the paint goes on smoothly and evenly, mix the second colour of emulsion paint with a little water to a creamy consistency.

❖ Free-hand checks can be simply created using a small mini-roller to make small squares of colour. For larger areas it may be worth the time and effort to draw up vertical guidelines to ensure the pattern runs straight.

❖ A softer, mottled pattern can be created by keeping the roller very dry and applying two colours over a white basecoat. Paint the wall and leave it to dry. Then work the first colour of squares with a roller, taking off excess paint on lining paper until a mottled image is achieved. When the first colour is dry, paint the squares in between with the second colour of paint.

YOU WILL NEED

Emulsion paint (2 colours)

Ruler

Coloured blackboard chalk

Long ruler or straight edge

Medium-sized paintbrush

Clean, lint-free cloth

WHAT TO DO

1 Paint the basecoat (to form one colour of the stripe) onto the wall. Leave to dry overnight.

2 Starting in one corner make the guidelines for your first stripe. To do this, use the ruler to measure the width of the stripe, and lightly mark the points with coloured blackboard chalk. Make four more marks further down the wall, and then join these up using the long ruler or straight edge. Repeat the process until the whole area to be painted is marked with stripes.

3 Charge the paintbrush with the second colour of emulsion paint and carefully paint in each alternate stripe. Work up to but do not touch the chalk lines you have drawn.

PRACTICAL POINTERS

❖ If your hand is a little unsteady or you want sharper edges to the stripes you can use a 3cm (1¹/₂in) wide masking tape as painting guidelines. Remove excess stickiness from the tape by attaching it to another surface and then peeling it off before fixing it to the wall. (This avoids any danger of lifting paint off when you remove it.) When the tape is properly in place, run a fingernail along the tape edges to ensure a good seal. Paint the stripes, taking the colour just over the edge of the tape. When you have finished a stripe, carefully peel the tape off the wall while the paint is still wet.

❖ For a softer striped effect use a sponging technique (see page 40) to apply the paint.

❖ Do not use too much paint on the roller at one time - take off any excess by rolling on a piece of lining paper.

❖ Use a paintbrush to transfer paint to the ridged area of the tray - charge your roller from here to stop paint getting on the edges of the roller.

❖ Try to complete one vertical line of stripes at a time to avoid 'joins' in the pattern.

❖ If the corners of your walls are not square, start stripes in the centre of each wall and work outwards. Use a plumb line to set your first vertical line.

❖ You can vary the width of the stripes by making more sections on a roller and by using a wider roller. Experiment with different effects trying each on a piece of lining paper before painting a wall.

4 After completing each stripe, carefully clean off any areas where the paint has gone over the guidelines using a moistened clean cloth.

5 Once the paint is dry, use a damp cloth to remove the chalk lines.

Above Rolling on the pattern. Here wavy stripes have been created by adapting an ordinary paint roller, and the harlequin checks have been made with a mini-roller.

PAINTED FURNITURE

If the idea of tackling a whole wall with a decorative paint effect is a bit daunting, you may find that a piece of furniture offers a more approachable project for you to get your teeth into.

Painted furniture has become a popular feature for any room in the home. Such pieces fit especially well in colour coordinated interiors and can serve as a useful linking device, incorporating colours from the walls, furnishings and flooring to lend a sense of cohesion to the finished room. As well as providing a decorative effect, paint also works as a wonderful camouflage, turning the most ordinary and unstylish piece into a visual delight.

Furniture made of soft wood such as pine is perfect for painting. Modern, glossy kitchen cupboards can be effectively transformed with paint, but sand down with sandpaper first to remove the shiny surface finish. Unless the piece is in bad shape, woods such as mahogany, cherry or elm should not be painted since the colour and markings of these are usually decorative enough in themselves. Oak is better stained or given a lime effect using a white or pale cream colour wash (see page 42).

Right A distressed paint effect finish tones down the spanking-new appearance of freshly painted furniture to fit with the atmosphere of this rustic scheme.

WHAT TO DO

1 For a successful finish, the wood or surface of the furniture must be properly prepared so that subsequent layers of paint will adhere to the surface. Strip off any varnish using paint stripper and wire wool, use methylated spirits and wire wool to remove French polish.

2 Old paint need only be stripped completely if it is badly chipped or wrinkled. Otherwise, simply rub down with sandpaper beginning with the coarse sandpaper and moving down to the fine grade. Take care to remove paint from any crevices and check that the edges are smooth and splinter free.

3 Fill and repair any cracks in the wood with the wood filler. For raw edges that need attention on furniture that will be well used, try a car body filler. Apply it in fine layers, and sand back until hard and smooth.

4 If there is bare wood, first paint on a coat of primer. Leave to dry.

5 Treat knots in wood with shellac to prevent them showing through when painted. Leave to dry.

6 Start with an undercoat, followed by two coats of emulsion or eggshell paint (if you are applying a decorative finish, these two coats should be in the basecoat colour that you have chosen for this). Rubbing down each layer of paint with sandpaper when | dry will give a better finish. For the last coat use a fine sandpaper dipped in water to prevent scratching on the surface.

7 After working your layer, or layers of decoration, finish with two coats of varnish.

YOU WILL NEED

Paint stripper or methylated spirits

Wire wool

Sandpaper (coarse, medium and fine grades)

Wood filler

Primer

Paintbrushes

Shellac

Emulsion or eggshell paint

Varnish

Below By incorporating different colours used in a room on wall units you can help to consolidate the different elements of a scheme.

BRIGHT IDEAS

❖ For a mellowed effect, add a touch of artist's oil colour in burnt umber to the final coat of varnish.

❖ Use any of the paint effects mentioned in this section of the book when painting furniture. Flat oil-based paint is harder wearing than emulsion paint and provides a thicker, protective cover for the wood underneath. Water-based emulsion paint works just as well but it must be varnished for durability.

❖ When painting, remember that two thin coats are better than one thick one. Always make sure each coat is completely dry before applying the next.

PAINTED FLOORS

Floors are a large part of any decorative scheme and yet, so often, the potential to be creative here is overlooked. Even when traditional floor coverings such as carpets or vinyl are swapped for the natural look of floor-boards, it's easy to forget that just like any other surface, there's plenty of scope to add a personal touch with decorative treatments. This could mean adding a hint of soft colour, or perhaps a fine stencilled border or even the more dramatic look of a chequerboard effect.

Decoration can also be a good foil for floorboards that really aren't quite up to scratch for being admired in their own right. Don't let the size of the surface put you off, since many ideas for floors are simple to do, and discreet enough not to impose on the rest of the colour and pattern in the room. Because floors take a lot of heavy-duty foot-work, varnish any decoration to protect it.

PREPARING WOOD FLOORS

Wooden floorboards must be thoroughly prepared for the best results. If you are painting the floor-boards with an all-over colour then you need only worry about achieving a smooth surface and sanding away any varnish. If you are planning to mix natural wood with pattern, for example a border stencil, the boards will need to be an even colour, and this will require more sanding.

If you are working in a small room, and the boards have not been treated you may be able to get away with sanding them by hand. However, invariably the simplest and quickest way to pre-pare wood floors is to hire a floor sander (ask at your local builder's merchants or DIY shop). Always wear protective clothing and face mask.

Right Not just for walking on, floors can be an important element of any scheme, whether you opt for subtle nuances of colour or bold dramatic statements.

WHAT TO DO

1 No matter how efficient the machine, this process creates an enormous amount of dust. Remove all the furniture from the room and anything else that can be taken out. Cover remaining items with dust sheets and block the cracks around the door with newspaper and open the windows. Check the floor for any protruding nails and hammer down into the surface.

2 Use a rough grade sandpaper on the drum and work diagonally across the floor, first in one direction and then the other. Roll the sander just as you would a lawn mower. When you have covered the main area of the floor switch to a fine grade of sandpaper and work up and down the length of the floorboards.

3 To finish the edges of the room (the sander won't be able to get that close) you will need a smaller, belt sander (also available to hire). Work in the direction of the floorboards.

4 Vacuum the room thoroughly. Remove any remaining dust with a piece of lint-free cloth soaked in white spirit.

BRIGHT IDEAS

❖ Rub paint into the bare boards to give a subtle hint of colour. Off-white or greyish tones will give the weathered and faded look of driftwood, use white for a simple bleached effect imitation or opt for a colour that has been used elsewhere in the scheme. If the natural colour of your floorboards is not so hot, use this technique as a base colour for stencilling.

Scrub the floor thoroughly before applying the paint (any thinned paint is suitable) along the grain of the wood over a 1m (1yd) square area at a time. Leave for a few minutes to allow the colour to soak into the wood, then wipe away the surface paint with a dry, lint-free cloth. If you are not intending to add decoration, seal the finish with two or three layers of polyurethane varnish, allowing each coat to dry thoroughly before applying the next.

❖ Stencilled motifs are an ideal decorative finish for floors. When drawing up your design don't forget to take into account other pattern and colour in the room. If the decor is already quite busy, a small discreet border may be enough and is less ambitious than attempting to stencil the whole floor. When you have completed the stencil seal the floor with two or three coats of polyurethane varnish.

❖ The stunning simplicity of checked floors works well in any scheme. Since the effect is hand-painted the pattern doesn't have to be absolutely accurate, but you will need to mark up the floor before you start. The effect is created by painting squares of one colour in a diamond pattern over a base coat colour so that together they create the finished chequerboard effect. Experiment with different combinations of colour and different sized squares to achieve the right balance. To do this, paint squares of card and try them out on the floor (you will need around five of each colour to give you an accurate impression of the finished effect).

PAINTING TEXTURED WALLCOVERINGS

Textured and relief patterned papers are a great half-way house between flat painted walls and the embellishment of an all-over printed pattern. For the novice wallpaper hanger, they can also be easier to work with, doing away with the need for complicated and accurate matching from one drop of paper to the next. Simple they may be, but that doesn't mean you can't have fun creating your own distinctive and original finish for any design that you choose.

PRACTICAL POINTERS

❖ Matt finish paints - either water-based emulsion or flat oil-based eggshell - will subdue the pattern of textured paper adding softness to walls without imposing on the rest of the scheme.

❖ Paints with a gloss finish such as vinyl silk emulsion, will highlight the pattern and make it sparkle on the walls.

❖ Add richness and depth to panels of relief patterned wallpapers - designed to imitate plasterwork - by finishing with a coat of polyurethane varnish.

❖ Relief patterned wallpapers can be imposing, so bear in mind the proportions and scale of the room when choosing a pattern.

❖ If your budget won't stretch to reinstating traditional cornicing, dado or picture rails, opt for relief patterned borders; they will fool even the keenest eye.

BRIGHT IDEAS

The texture of the paper you choose can be enhanced or subdued depending on the type of paint you use - a matt finish, such as that of water-based matt emulsion paint, will play down the texture, and is excellent for covering woodchip paper. A shiny finish, on the other hand, such as vinyl silk emulsion, will highlight the raised areas and make more of figurative or floral motifs that are designed to be noticed. One of the simplest ways to add interest and impact to fail-safe colour options such as white and cream is to set plain painted walls against textured paper. Run the paper up to dado rail height only, and paint with vinyl silk emulsion - you'll find it is instantly eye catching without imposing on the rest of the decor. Dividing walls into bands in this way offers the perfect opportunity to introduce a second colour into your decor. Choose a bold contrast and transform it into a decorative focal point, or opt for the discreet sophistication of a closely toning shade.

Just as printed patterns can be mixed together as wallpaper and borders, so the same can be done with textured papers. Mix a small all-over pattern with a more strident border (just as you might printed pattern) and choose different shades of colour to accentuate the effect.

Arguably the most elegant - and certainly the most traditional - embossed papers are those known as Anaglypta and Lincrusta which are designed to imitate plasterwork. The raised surface design can be used as a canvas for all sorts of creative ideas with paint and colour. A coat of high gloss paint is the simplest way to bring out the pattern, or you could add a mellowed antique appearance by using a distressing paint technique (see page 44) where a darker shade of glaze is applied over a base coat and then wiped away from the raised areas to create patches of light and dark shading.

If you have a steady hand and the time to spare, you can use these relief wallcoverings to create the illusion of real plasterwork on your walls by painting over the raised design only, in a contrasting colour to the base. This works best on plain painted walls. Choose either a frieze or patterned border with traditional, architectural plasterwork motifs. Hang the frieze or border on the wall and when the paper has dried, paint to match the walls and allow to dry. Using a fine artist's paintbrush, pick out the raised areas of pattern with white or stone coloured beige emulsion paint (either matt or vinyl silk). This will take a while and a lot of concentration, but the effect is well worth it.

Above A mouthwatering mix of colours helps to highlight the contrasts of pattern between an Anaglypta wallcovering and border, creating a distinctive look for these bathroom walls.

WALLPAPER BORDERS

Wallpaper borders were originally used to conceal the tacks that held wallpaper in position. Of course, today they are purely decorative which means they need no longer be relegated to just the edges of a wallspace and can even be turned into a feature in themselves.

Above *Dividing a wall with different treatments of colours can leave it looking cold and disjointed; by choosing a border that contains shades of both you can turn disparate elements into a winning team.*

POSITION OF BORDERS

Borders can be used as a device to create natural bands of area on the wall. These sections may be of different colours, or one area can be painted while the other is patterned. Likewise, the position of a border on a wall can reduce or increase the height of a room. Use them towards the centre of a wall and the eye is drawn downwards and the ceiling appears lower, position them in place of a picture rail and the opposite effect is created.

Because borders attract the eye they can also be used to highlight particular features in a room. By running a simple border around the edge of a fireplace or doorframe, for example, it will be brought into prominence.

PRACTICAL POINTERS

❖ Experiment with different positions for borders - use reusable adhesive to temporarily keep the border in place.

❖ Use strong coloured borders against small patterned wallpaper to lend a sense of order and definition.

❖ Make sure you don't use too much of the border so that it conflicts with pattern elsewhere in the room. Experimenting with different positions should help you avoid this.

❖ Use a border to draw attention to a decorative feature or detail in a room, such as vertical stripes on either side of a fireplace, or a panel around a picture or mirror.

Left A pale, small patterned paper was in danger of being overwhelmed by the surrounding cornucopia of bold motifs. So, to redress the balance, a coordinating border of stronger blue was added.

BRIGHT IDEAS

❖ Use the border to create patterned panels in a room. Panels are easy to do and are a useful way to break up plain walls. Use a single panel to frame a picture, or you could create a whole panelled room with squares or rectangles of border You can also use this effect to give small patterned wallpapers a sense of order. Choose a border in a stronger colour with clean, simple lines. The key to the success of the panel treatment is making neat, mitred corners (see page 75).

❖ Another idea is to 'fill' the panel with contrasting or coordinating paper. For example, in a small bedroom an all-over pattern might be too much, but plain walls would be too cold, so a floral pattern used sparingly in this way can introduce instant country cottage charm without being overpowering. Work out the position and size of each panel using reusable adhesive to keep the border in place. Measure the width and height of the area in the middle and cut a piece of patterned wallpaper a little larger than this (so there will be an overlap between the border and the paper). Hang the patterned paper in place and then hang the border on top.

DECOUPAGE

Découpage is the art of using cut-out motifs or illustrations to create decorative effects and is a way of giving printed pattern an unusual and original twist. There is now a huge range of pre-cut printed paper motifs available which are designed to be used as decoration. They range from the floral to trompe l'oeil illusions of fabric and architectural designs and are a quick way to add delightful ornamentation to the decor. And, of course, you can make your own cut-outs from wallpapers or borders.

Below Make yourself some individual style by cutting out print room motifs and ornamentation and create your own decorative gallery. A monochrome trompe l'oeil border completes the traditional scene.

The print rooms of the eighteenth century where a collector would arrange black and white engravings to create a wall of different images is being revived as a decorative treatment. But instead of collecting the pictures, tricks with printed paper are being used to create the effect in a much simpler, and less expensive, way. Ranges of specially designed copies of prints, complete with frames and decorative swags and tassels for display, are available to buy from a number of suppliers.

Cut-out motifs can be sourced from anywhere (since the paper is varnished, you do not have to worry about its durability). Wrapping paper provides a wealth of material and is relatively cheap and easy to collect.

WHAT TO DO

1 Make sure the surface you are applying the motifs to is clean and grease-free and that any paint or decorative finish you have worked is dry.

2 Spread the cut-out motifs onto a table so that you can see all the different colours, shapes and sizes at a glance (you will find this helpful when looking for a particular colour or size of picture you need to fill a gap).

3 Place the images on the surface you are decorating and experiment with different arrangements. If you are creating an all-over pattern, overlap the edges of one image onto another to ensure there is no surface

underneath showing through.

4 Leave the arrangement for a while and go back to it from time to time - you'll be surprised how suddenly colour combinations that don't work together suddenly leap out at you when you look at it with a fresh eye. Use a sheet of glass or clear object to keep the paper in place.

5 Once you are happy with the arrangement stick the images in place. Mix the paste or adhesive according to instructions on the packet.

6 It's a good idea to try and stick the images in layers. Apply those that are most hidden first, and then build up the cut-outs until you finally apply those that will be on top. Stick down the images lightly so that they can be lifted again without tearing paper underneath if you need to reposition them. Try not to use too much paste on the paper.

7 When you are happy with the effect, apply more pressure to the paper to ensure the cut-outs are well stuck down. Use a dry cloth to wipe away carefully any paste that oozes onto the surface, and

YOU WILL NEED

Collection of cut-out paper images

Wallpaper paste or appropriate glue

Glue brush

Shellac or polyurethane varnish

Medium-sized paintbrush

Artist's oil paint in burnt umber

BRIGHT IDEAS

❖ Decide on a theme for your découpage treatment and begin collecting images - don't cut them out at this stage since the edges might get worn.

❖ If a wall of prints sounds too much you could opt for one or two on a small area (perhaps above a fireplace) instead.

❖ Be as creative, imaginative and wacky with your choice of images as you like. For example, you may choose to cover a photograph album of a particular holiday with paper artefacts and souvenirs from the trip such as bus tickets, or postcards.

❖ Spread all the cut-out images on a table so you can see at a glance what you've got.

❖ Once the arrangement is in place leave for a while and go back to it from time to time, fiddling with small details until you are happy with the appearance.

dab the edges of the top motifs so that the surface is flat. Leave until the paper is dry. If any of the edges come away, simply use a small brush and a dab of glue to seal them back down again.

8 Use the paintbrush to apply the varnish, taking care not to catch the edges of the cut-outs. The effect is best when many thin layers of varnish are applied - about five or six will give a good depth to the surface. Make sure each layer is dry before applying the next. Tint the last coat of varnish with a little artist's oil paint in burnt umber to give a mellowed, slightly aged effect.

BASICS

Having decided on the pattern and colour for your scheme and thought about ways in which you might like to use them, now comes the truly exciting part of decorating - putting ideas into action.

If taken step by step, decorating can be relatively straightforward but careful planning is the key. Think through every part of the decoration before you begin to put colour and pattern into place. For no matter how new your home, or how well-maintained the walls and woodwork are, no two rooms are exactly the same and are rarely ever a simple box of clean straight lines. You will doubtless come across one or two situations for which there are no hard and fast answers. You may find, for example, that one corner doesn't run parallel with the rest of the room, or when hanging a border that the wall heights vary slightly. It's better to tackle such situations in advance rather than discovering as you go - this will slow down the work and could cause you to waste materials and time.

The information in this chapter may not have all the answers but it will give you the basics to be able to deal with these small hiccups. Take every stage in turn and instead of a daunting task you'll find it enjoyable and fun as you watch the results of all your hard work and ideas literally unfold before your eyes.

Right *Seeing how your creative ideas help to transform the appearance of a room makes all the hard work of planning and preparation well worth the effort.*

PREPARING SURFACES FOR DECORATION:
What's what
Practical pointers
Preparing walls
Preparing woodwork
Preparing radiators

PAINTING:
What's what
Calculating the amount of paint you need
Applying paint
Painting with a brush
Painting with a roller
Painting ceilings and walls
Painting woodwork
Painting radiators
Cleaning brushes
Practical pointers

WALLPAPERING:
You will need
Calculating the amount of wallpaper you need
Practical pointers
Lining paper
Hanging wallpaper
Papering ceilings
Hanging borders
Practical pointers

PREPARING SURFACES FOR DECORATION

The ally of any professional decorator is the thorough and careful preparation of surfaces. Prepared surfaces provide a key for the new layer of decoration to adhere to, ensuring good and long-lasting results. In many cases this is not as labour intensive as it might sound, but where extra elbow-grease is required, the rewards of a perfect finish will more than amply repay the effort.

WHAT'S WHAT

There is a vast range of tools for decorating preparation, each designed to make a specific job easier. You may find that you need only a few for the room you are working on. But remember, these tools do last and will doubtless be useful again in the future so are worth the investment where necessary.

Scrapers Used for removing wallpaper and paint. You should have at least two, a wide one for main areas of a wall and a narrower one for dealing with paintwork and detail areas.

Shavehooks A hooked scraper, specially designed for getting into the indented parts of mouldings. You will probably need one of these if you need to remove thick paint from grooved or panelled woodwork or plasterwork.

Sandpapers An abrasive paper used for creating a smooth surface and providing a key for paint to adhere to. You will need varying grades, being coarse, medium and fine. Wet and dry paper can be used wet for a finish with no scratches. If you have trouble working with a sheet of paper, you may find a wooden block which holds the paper firmly, easier to handle.

Bucket and sponge To wash down walls and paintwork.

A dry wide paintbrush For removing dust. Wire bristles are good for metal such as radiators.

Paint stripping material Either a hot air stripper, blow torch or liquid paintstripper. Any of these would be used for removing larger areasof problem paint.

Dust sheets To protect furnishings in the room you are decorating.

Step ladder For reaching high areas of walls and the ceilings. Make sureit is safe and sturdy.

Filler and filling knives To repair and make good cracks and damaged areas of plaster and woodwork. Use an all-purpose filler for larger cracks and a fine filler for small cracks. You will need an appropriate size knife to apply the filler depending on the size of the area you are working on.

PREPARING WALLS

PAINTED WALLS

Scrape off any flaking paint and smooth the surface with sandpaper. Wash down with soapy water (working down the wall) and lightly rub down gloss-painted walls with fine sandpaper to provide a key. Rinse off any dust and allow to dry overnight.

NEWLY PLASTERED WALLS

Plaster must be clean and dry (leave for 4-6 months to dry out before decorating). Rub off any surface salt with a dry cloth. Some newly plastered walls may need a primer, check with your builder.

WALLPAPERED WALLS

Whether wallpapering again or painting, for the best finish you should aim to remove any existing wallcovering.

❖ Regular wallpapers (not washable, vinyl or textured coverings) can be removed by soaking the wall with water. Mix a little washing-up liquid in the water and apply liberally to the wall with a sponge. The paper should be left to allow the water to soften the paste. Score the surface with a scraper and try to remove the paper. If it is difficult to remove, wait a little longer.

❖ Washable wallpapers are non-absorbent, so you need to scratch the surface with a serrated scraper to allow the water to seep through to the back. Soak the paper as before and leave until the paste has softened. When you remove vinyl paper you may find a backing is left behind; professionals recommend you remove this too, in the same way as for regular wallpaper.

❖ If you have large areas of stubborn wallpaper it may be worth hiring a steam stripper (ask at your local DIY shop or builder's merchants). This uses steam to dampen the paper, encouraging it to peel off the wall.

❖ Textured coatings are difficult to remove. Check with the manufacturer or supplier for recommended methods.

❖ Remove any remaining flecks of paper with a wet scrubbing brush or sandpaper.

FILLING CRACKS

1 Open up small cracks with a putty knife or the end of a screwdriver to make them easier to fill. For larger cracks, remove any loose material and cut back plaster to a firm edge.

2 Dust down the crack with a brush and fill with a few fine layers of all-purpose filler (rather than one thick one). Use a narrow-bladed filling knife and push the filler deep into the crack. Allow each layer to dry thoroughly before applying the next one.

3 When the filler is dry, sand back to make a smooth surface with the wall. Wash the wall to remove any dust. Allow the wall to dry overnight before decorating.

PREPARING WOODWORK

PROBLEM AREAS WITH WALLS

❖ Dampness - do not paint or paper over damp. The only solution is to find the root of the problem and get it treated.

❖ Mould growth - often the result of a build up of condensation; improving ventilation in the room will help. Treat the affected area with a mould cleaner, applied with a sponge. Use rubber gloves to protect your hands and allow to dry as in the manufacturer's instructions.

PAINTED WOODWORK

If the paintwork is sound, rub it with a fine sandpaper to provide a key for the next layer of paint and wash it down. Wet and dry paper (an abrasive paper which can be used wet or dry) can be used wet to prevent scratches on the surface. Remove any flaking bits of paint and sand back to a smooth surface.

STRIPPING PAINT

If paint is badly chipped or cracked, or looks uneven due to too many layers of paint, you may need to remove it from the wood. A blow torch or hot air stripper heats and softens the paint making it possible to remove with a scraper. Work on a small area at a time, and move the heat source continually to prevent scorch marks on the wood. If the wood is not to be painted again, use paint stripper. It takes more time but it is effective. Also use paint stripper to remove paint from intricate beading and architraves. A shavehook will help, but for very fine areas you may even need to use a stiff toothbrush to get into all the crevices.

NEW WOODWORK

Sand down any rough edges or splinters, rounding off the rough edges. If the wood has many knots in it, paint these over with shellac to prevent them showing through. Fill cracks and joints with a wood filler and then sand down to a smooth surface when dry. Wash off any dust and allow to dry. All new wood should be primed to reduce its absorbency and provide a key for the paint.

PREPARING RADIATORS

Dust away any metal scrapings on new radiators and apply an appropriate primer. On painted radiators, remove any loose rust or paint with a wire bristled brush or scraper (use a primer on any bare metal patches that appear). Sand down the paint to provide a key for the new layer.

PAINTING

Paint is the easiest of decorating materials to apply. But the better the surface, the better the finished result, so preparation is of paramount importance. Work in a clean, dust-free room, covering all furnishings with protective covers. Professionals recommend a lining paper (see page 72 for hanging details) as the base for painted walls, and if there is any unevenness in the plasterwork this will give the best finish. However, if your walls are smooth, you can paint straight onto plaster. All the painting should be completed before hanging decorative wallcoverings.

CALCULATING THE AMOUNT OF PAINT YOU NEED

Different types of paint cover different amounts of surface area (see page 19). Amounts are given in terms of one litre per sq m (sq yd) area.

To work out the size of the area you are intending to cover, measure the length of each wall and multiply by the height (this gives you the sq m [sq yd] area). Add together the measurements for each wall and the ceiling (if it is to be painted in the same colour) to determine the total surface area to be painted.

Then, to work out how many litres of paint you will need, divide the total surface area by the area covered by the type of paint you are choosing.

Repeat the process for all separate areas such as woodwork and doors. Remember to take into account how many coats you will need.

Choose the recommended type of paint for the area of the room you are painting. Although decorating rules are made to be broken, it is advisable to follow guidelines unless you are an experienced decorator. In general, paint walls with either water-based emulsion paint or flat oil-based eggshell paint, and use oil-based paints on woodwork. Never use a different type of paint over another while still wet. Always follow manufacturer's guidelines for undercoats.

WHAT'S WHAT

Paint roller Good for applying paint to larger areas and for use on ceilings. Use a deep pile roller for textured surfaces, a medium pile for smoother surfaces.

Paint tray To hold paint for roller application.

Brushes Available in different widths, narrow brushes (2.5-5cm [1-2in]), are good for finishing off around edges, windows and for applying gloss paints. Wider brushes (up to 15cm [6in]), are needed for applying emulsion to walls (if you don't use a roller).

Masking tape Used to protect areas and edges that should not be painted. Use tape that is 3.5cm (1 $\frac{1}{2}$in) wide and stick it around frames on windows and where one colour meets another, such as around the top of skirting boards. It can be peeled off easily without leaving a sticky residue.

A clean cloth To remove any stray spots of paint.

Cleaning solution Water-based paints can be cleaned off brushes in warm soapy water, oil-based paints should be cleaned in white spirit.

Two step ladders Use these for painting ceiling.s Have a stout plank between them fixed at an appropriate height.

APPLYING PAINT

You will find it easier to paint different areas of the room in a certain order - this minimises the chances of a completed area being splashed with another colour of paint, and of you having to work close to an area that is still wet. The recommended order in which to paint is: 1 ceilings, 2 walls, 3 radiators and all woodwork except skirting boards, 4 skirting boards.

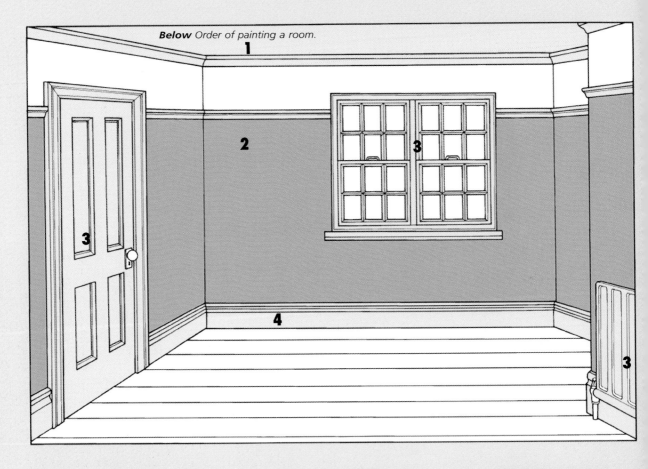

Below Order of painting a room.

PAINTING WITH A BRUSH

Using a brush to apply paint gives more control over the medium and should be used for the corners and edges of rooms and paintwork. Using a brush for large areas will take longer than a roller, but some people prefer to work this way.

1 Ensure the bristles are dry and clean.

2 Dip up to one-third of the bristles in the paint to load the brush. The brush should not be dripping with paint, wipe away any excess on a string tied across the top of the paint can.

3 Hold the brush like a pen, using a loose wrist action to move it up and down.

PAINTING WITH A ROLLER

Rollers are useful for covering main areas of walls and ceilings quickly and evenly.

1 Tip some paint into the paint tray. To load the roller, rock it backwards and forwards in the paint tray pushing it up to the top of the ridged slope to remove excess paint. Take care not to overload with paint.

2 Apply with criss-cross strokes to the wall, ensuring a smooth start and finish. Removing the roller suddenly may cause splashes.

PAINTING CEILINGS AND WALLS

1 If you are using lining paper on the walls or ceiling, make sure this is dry and you are happy with the finish before applying paint.

2 Apply a thinned first coat of paint to walls and ceilings (whether lined or not), using water for water-based emulsion, white spirit for flat oil-based paint such as eggshell. This will reduce the absorbency of the surface and give a better finish to the colour. Apply the paint in random brush strokes to give an even distribution of colour.

3 For the top coat, start by painting a band of paint around the edges of the ceiling using a 5cm (2in)-wide brush. Paint a similar band of colour around doorways, windows, light switches and fireplaces and along the top of the skirting board.

4 Fill in the rest of the areas in blocks of about 2 sq m (2 sq yd) working first the ceiling and then the walls. Continue to the next block while the previous one is still wet and overlap the colour slightly to blend the areas together. Always complete whole sections, such as one wall or a ceiling, at a time.

5 When applying paint with a paintbrush, work in different directions over the same area to avoid noticeable brush marks and create an even colour. Do not overcharge the brush with paint. If using a roller, apply the paint in criss-cross strokes. To prevent splashes, sweep the roller off the surface, rather than lifting it abruptly.

PAINTING WOODWORK

1 Apply an undercoat if required and leave it to dry as instructed by the manufacturers.

2 For the top coat colour, start by applying paint along the grain of the wood. Cover small areas at a time, 30 sq cm (12 sq in) panels or a strip of skirting about 60 cm (24 in) long, without recharging the brush. Then dip the brush in the paint again and apply a little more paint with crossways strokes. Finish by stroking the paint along the grain again. Use only upward strokes if the grain runs vertically.

3 When painting panelled doors, remove the door furniture (eg handles, knobs and key plates) first (1). The recommended order to paint is then: 2 the mouldings, 3 panels, 4 vertical bars, 5 horizontal bars, 6 door frame.

4 Mask the glass on windows with masking tape. Leave a 3mm ($1/_8$in) margin between the glass and wood for a small overlap of paint onto the window, so sealing any cracks and preventing moisture seeping in behind the paint. Do not paint primer or undercoat onto the glass. Paint the window bars first, then the surround of the actual window, and finally the window frame.

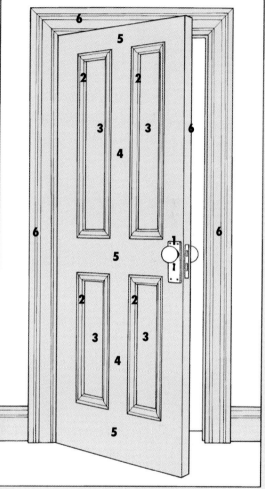

Remove the masking tape when the paint is dry to the touch. Remove any paint splashes on the glass with a scalpel or razor blade.

5 Roll back flooring before painting skirting boards. If this is not possible, protect with a wide band of masking tape around the edge. Begin in the corner of the room and complete one wall section at a time. Remove the masking tape when the paint is dry.

PAINTING RADIATORS

1   Allow the radiator to cool completely before painting.

2   Use a coloured paint as a first coat to guard against any dis-colouration which can occur with pale-coloured paints when the radiator heats up. Keep bleed valves free of paint.

CLEANING BRUSHES

It is well worth getting into the habit of cleaning your brushes as soon as you have finished for the day. For water-based paints use detergent, or for oil-based paints use white spirit. Dry carefully using kitchen paper.

PRACTICAL POINTERS

❖ Open tins of paint carefully so that dust from the lid does not get into the paint. Always stir well.

❖ Do not overcharge your brush or roller with paint. Remember that two thin coats of paint are better than one thick one.

❖ Complete one section of a room at a time, such as a wall or the whole ceiling.

❖ When painting on an absorbent surface such as bare plaster or lining paper, thin the first coat of paint - use water for water-based emulsions, white spirit for flat oil-based paints such as eggshell.

❖ Always allow one coat of paint to dry thoroughly before applying the next.

❖ If you want to take a break during painting, wrap brushes in tin foil to keep them moist and prevent the paint from drying. Do not leave them like this for a long period of time.

WALLPAPERING

For most inexperienced decorators, hanging wallpaper is one of the ultimate decorating challenges. Although it needs to be worked carefully, it is not as difficult as the finished effect might lead you to believe. Make sure you have plenty of space to work in, and all the equipment ready and easily to hand. If the paper has a large pattern repeat, decide whereabouts towards the top of the wall you want to start it.

YOU WILL NEED

Plumb line and bob

Tape measure

Coloured blackboard chalk

Wide pasting brush

Wallpaper paste

Bucket to keep the paste in

Wallpaper smoothing brush

Pair of long-bladed scissors

Seam roller

Pasting table or suitable surface at least 53cm (21in) wide and 1.5m (5ft) long

CALCULATING THE AMOUNT OF WALLPAPER YOU NEED

The amount of wallpaper you need will depend on the height and width of your walls, the size of the printed pattern and the width of the wallpaper.

1 Measure the length around the room, excluding major obstacles such as large picture windows or built-in cupboards, but including doors and ordinary windows. This measurement is the perimeter of your room.

2 Measure the height of the wall from the skirting board to the picture rail or cornicing, depending on where you intend to stop the wallpaper. If there is a large pattern repeat, add on the amount you need to allow from one drop to the next - it may be as much as a whole pattern length. Divide the total measurement into the length of the roll of wallpaper you have chosen. The answer tells you how many drops you can get from one roll.

3 Divide the total perimeter of the wall by the width of the wallpaper. This will tell you how many drops of wallpaper it will take to complete the room.

4 Now divide the number of drops needed by the number of drops you can get from a roll. This will tell you how many rolls you need.

PRACTICAL POINTERS

❖ Make sure all the rolls of wallpaper are from the same batch number.

❖ It is advisable to buy an extra roll of wallpaper, in case you make any mistakes or for any repairs you might need to make in the future.

❖ Before you start papering, unwrap every roll and check for any imperfections.

❖ Don't assume wallpaper will come off the roll the right way up. In fact, the opposite is quite common.

❖ Always use the same strength of paste for the lining paper (if you use it) and top paper.

❖ Always work from the top of the wall down, and paste from the top of the drop to the bottom.

LINING PAPER

Although professionals invariably use lining paper before wallpapering, it is not necessary unless the wall surface is very poor and uneven. Lining paper that is to be wallpapered over should be hung across the room - known as cross-lining.

Use the following instructions for pasting and cutting, but start at the top of the wall, and run the paper horizontally across it.

Line one wall at a time and work downwards towards the skirting. You will probably need to cut the final strip of paper to fit the remaining area of wall. Measure at various points along the wall and use the widest point as your guide. Allow 5cm (2in) extra for trimming. Make sure the lining paper is dry before hanging the top paper; this could take up to a couple of days. Use the same strength of paste for the lining and top papers. If you are going to paint lining paper, hang as for ordinary wallpaper.

HANGING WALLPAPER

1 Start papering near a door or window so that any slight mismatching when you come to the end of the papering will not be so noticeable. To set a vertical line for the first drop of paper, cover the plumb line in coloured chalk and hang it from the ceiling, close to the wall. Hold the weight in place and gently snap the string to create a soft chalk line on the wall.

2 Mix the paste according to the instructions on the packet. Measure up and cut the first drop, allowing at least 10cm (4in) extra for trimming. Place right side down on the pasting table with one edge of the paper overlapping the edge of the table slightly to prevent paste getting onto the table. Apply the paste with the pasting brush working from the top of the drop, down the length of the table from the centre out towards the side overlapping the edge of the table. Then shift the paper to the other edge of the table and apply paste on that side in the same way.

3 To move the paper down the table, fold over the pasted end in an S-shape. Apply paste to the remaining length of paper. Leave the past-

ed paper to rest according to the manufacturer's instructions so the paste can soak in.

4 Fold the pasted surfaces together bringing the top and bottom to meet in the middle (you can also use concertina folds). Check which is the top end of the length. Carry the folded paper over one arm to the wall.

5 Hold the top corners and open the top fold. Position the top edge so that it is about 5cm (2in) above the edge of the cornice or picture rail ensuring one edge matches the plumbed line and stick the top half of the length onto the wall. Gently slide the paper into the exact position.

6 Smooth down the middle of the paper with the wallpaper smoothing brush, working outwards towards the edges to remove the wrinkles and air bubbles as you go. Do not apply too much pressure as this might stretch the paper and take care not to get any paste on the right side of the paper. If bubbles and wrinkles appear, lift the paper away from the wall and smooth down again.

7 Unfold the rest of the paper and continue to smooth down as you go, leaving a 5cm (2in) trimming margin at the bottom of the wall.

8 When the whole drop is in place and you are happy with the finish, mark the trimming line at the top by drawing the back of the scissors along the angle between the cornice or picture rail and the wall. Peel the paper back from the wall slightly and trim along the marked line. Repeat at the skirting. Wipe away any excess paste from the ceiling or skirting with a damp sponge, and brush down the edges of the paper.

9 Cut the next length of paper allowing extra at the top for pattern matching if necessary. Paste and fold as before. Place it beside the first length of paper, and unfold the top half as before, matching the pattern at eye level. Stick it to the wall, sliding the paper exactly into position. Smooth down the rest of the drop. When you are happy with the

second drop of paper, gently run the seam roller down the seams to ensure they are well stuck down. Don't roll embossed or relief papers.

10 Never hang a full width of paper around an inside corner - always hang it in two parts. Measure the distance from the last piece you have hung to the corner at several points and then use the widest point as your guide.

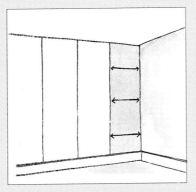

11 Cut a strip of paper 2.5cm (1in) wider than this distance, paste and hang it with the extra 2.5cm (1in) overlapping onto the next wall. Cut into the overlap if necessary to help smooth out any bulges. Measure the width of the offcut left over from the corner drop and use the plumb line to mark a vertical line the same distance from the side wall. Paste and hang the off-

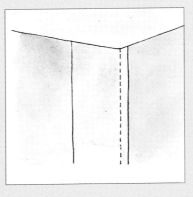

cut, aligning the uncut edge with the vertical line so that the cut edge fits flush in the corner. Use the same technique to wrap paper around external corners.

12 To paper around light switches and plug sockets, first turn off the electricity at the mains. Hang the paper in the normal way smoothing it gently over the fitting. Cut into the paper at the centre of the switch or socket and then make four diagonal cuts to 2.5cm (1in) beyond each corner. Unscrew the fitting slightly and tuck the edges under the faceplate.

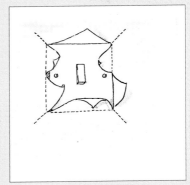

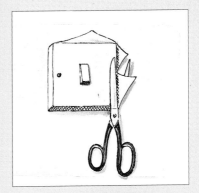

13 When fitting paper around doors and windows, cut away the waste paper to make it easier to handle.

PAPERING CEILINGS

1 Mark a straight line across the ceiling to align the paper against. Make a mark from the wall at either end of the length and then join up the two points using chalk covered string pinned taughtly in position. Snap the string to leave a mark on the ceiling as a guide for the first strip of paper.

2 Paste the paper as for wallpaper, and then make neat concertina folds for easy handling.

3 Use scaffolding planks and two ladders to create a raised platform to stand on when papering. Make sure it is at a comfortable height for you to reach the ceiling.

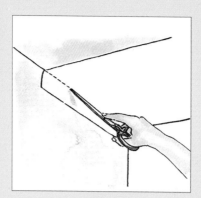

4 Paste the paper as for the wall, leaving a 5cm (2in) overlap at one end and gently unfolding, sticking and smoothing out the sections of paper as you work your way down the length of the ceiling, checking that the paper is flush with the chalk guideline.

5 If there is a ceiling light, remove the bulb and shade and turn off the electricity at the mains. Smooth the paper over the fitting and make a cut in the centre. Clip at regular intervals around the fitting, unscrew it slightly and tuck the edge of the paper underneath.

Left You needn't feel restricted to hanging borders around rooms - here strips of border have been used to highlight a wall decoration.

HANGING BORDERS

Whether you use borders to finish walls or create decorative panels, you need to plan carefully where they will go before pasting them to the wall. Corners should be mitred, and it's worth doing a couple of practice mitres to work out where to position the corner in terms of the pattern and to check that it matches accurately. If you are sticking borders to a vinyl wallpaper use a specially formulated overlap and repair adhesive (ask your supplier for advice). Otherwise, use the same strength of paste as for the wallpaper. Measure the length of wall to be covered with border pattern and use this to work out how many rolls you need - most come in 3.3m (11yd) rolls, but check on the package first.

WHAT TO DO

1 Plan the position of the borders carefully. Stick lengths in place with reusable adhesive and try out different positions and heights before making a final decision. On plain walls or paper use the spirit level to mark a horizontal and then use the batten or rule

YOU WILL NEED

Reusable adhesive

Spirit level

Straight edge

Coloured blackbroad chalk

Plumb line (optional)

Wallpaper table

Wallpaper paste

Bucket for the paste

Wallpaper smoothing brush

Wet sponge

Metal ruler

Piece of card 18 sq cm
(7 sq in)

Trimming knife

to draw in guidlines around the room. For panelled effects, you will need to mark a vertical line using the plumb line. If the ceiling is uneven you may need to adjust the horizontal so that the border looks straight to the eye in relation to the room. When applying borders to pattern wallpapers, use a motif on the paper as your horizontal guide.

2 Lay the wallpaper border face down on the pasting table and paste down the length, working out to the edges. Wipe down the table after each pasting to keep it clean.

3 Fold the pasted border into a concertina that you can hold comfortably in your hand. Position the border in place, stick a section to the wall and start to smooth the paper in place using the wallpaper smoothing brush and taking care to follow guidelines or patterns as appropriate. Wipe off any paste which oozes out from the edges of the border with a damp sponge.

4 To work the mitred corners paste one strip of paper in place leaving an over-

lap of about 15cm (6in) beyond the corner. Cut the second strip of paper again with an overlap of 15cm (6in) beyond the corner. Paste the second strip in place. While the paper is still wet, gently lift the ends of the strips at the corner and place a piece of card underneath. Place the paper back down in position. Using the metal ruler and a pencil, draw a diagonal line from the top corner where the two strips overlap, down to where the two strips meet on the inside corner. Cut through both layers of paper using the sharp knife, drawing the blade down along the metal edge for a clean line. Remove the offcuts of paper and gently lift the border away from the wall to remove the backing. Smooth the border back in place.

STOCKISTS AND SUPPLIERS

Paint

Laura Ashley
256-8 Regent Street
Oxford Circus
London W1R 5DA
(for local branch stockists telephone 01628 770345)

JW Bollom & JT Keep
PO Box 78
Croydon Road
Beckenham
Kent
BR3 4BL
Telephone: 0181 658 2299

Crown Paints at DIY stores nationwide
(for local stockists and further information telephone the Crown Paints Advice Line on 01254 704951)

Dulux (ICI Paints) at DIY stores nationwide
(for local stockists and further information telephone the Dulux Advice Centre on 01753 550555)

Farrow & Ball Ltd
(For colour cards and information contact 01202 876141. Mail order)

Paint Service Co Ltd
19 Eccleston Street
London SW1W 9LX
Telephone: 0171 730 6408

Papers & Paints
4 Park Walk
London SW10 OAD
Telephone: 0171 352 8626
(paint stockists and will mix colours to order)

The Shaker Shop
322 King's Road
London SW3 5UH
Telephone: 0171 352 3918

Spectrum Paint by Sanderson
112-120 Brompton Road
London SW3 1JJ
(for local stockists telephone 0171 584 3344)

Specialist materials for paint effects and decorative treatments

JW Bollom & JT Keep
PO Box 78
Croydon Road
Beckenham
Kent BR3 4BL
Telephone: 0181 658 2299

L Cornelissen & Son Ltd
105 Great Russell Street
London WC1B 3RY
Telephone: 0171 636 1045
(mail order)

Paint Magic
116 Sheen Road
Richmond
Surrey
TW9 1UR
Telephone: 0181 940 5503
(mail order)

Paint Service Co Ltd
19 Eccleston Street
London SW1W 9LX
Telephone: 0171 730 6408

Stencils and decorative paper treatments

National Trust Enterprises Ltd, (Print Room Borders)
PO Box 101
Melksham
Wiltshire SN12 8EA
Telephone: 01225 705676
(print room borders available through mail order. Also available from selected National Trust shops)

Ornamenta (trompe l'oeil wallpaper decorations and borders)
PO Box 784
London SW7 2TB
Telephone: 0171 584 3857
(trompe l'oeil wallpaper decorations and borders available through mail order)

Paint Magic (stencils)
116 Sheen Road
Richmond
Surrey TW9 1UR
Telephone: 0181 940 5503
(mail order)

Pavilion (stencils)
6A Howe Street
Edinburgh EH3 6TD
Telephone: 0131 225 3590
(mail order)

The Stencil Library
Stocksfield Hall
Stockfield
Northumberland NE43 7TN
Telephone: 01661 844 844
(mail order)

The Stencil Store
91 Lower Sloane Street
London
SW1W 8DA
Telephone: 0171 730 0728
(for details of other branches telephone 01923 285577. Mail order)

Wallpapers

Anaglypta wallcoverings
Crown Berger Ltd
(for local stockists telephone 01254 704951)

Laura Ashley
256-8 Regent Street
Oxford Circus
London W1R 5DA
(for local branch stockists telephone 01628 770345)

GP & J Baker
(for local stockists telephone
01494 467467)

Jane Churchill Interiors
151 Sloane Street
London SW1X 9BX
Telephone: 0171 730 9847
(for local stockists telephone
0181 874 6484)

Cole & Son
144 Offord Road
London N1 1NS
Telephone: 0171 607 4288

Colefax and Fowler
39 Brook Street
London W1Y 2JE
Telephone: 0171 493 2231
(for local stockists telephone
0181 874 6484)

Coloroll
(for local stockists telephone
01282 617777)

Designers Guild
267 and 277 Kings Road
London SW3 5EN
(for local stockists telephone
0171 243 7300)

Anna French
343 King's Road
London SW3 5ES
(for local stockists telephone
0171 351 1126)

Marks & Spencers
(for local branch stockists telephone 0171 935 4422

Muriel Short Designs
Hewitts Estate
Elmbridge Road
Cranleigh
Surrey GU6 8LW
Telephone: 01483 271211

Osborne & Little
304-308 King's Road
London SW3 5UH
Telephone: 0171 352 1456

(for local stockists telephone
0181 675 2255)

Ramm Son & Crocker
26 Chelsea Design Centre
Lots Road
London SW10 OXE
(for local stockists telephone
0171 352 0931)

Sanderson
112-120 Brompton Road
London SW3 1JJ
Telephone: 0171 584 3344

Turner Wallcoverings
(for local stockists telephone
0171 609 4201)

Brian Yates
(for local stockists telephone
01524 35035)

INDEX

Page numbers in *italics* represent illustrations

A

Arts and Crafts wallpaper, *33*
assessing wallpaper design, 26-7

B

base coat, 39
bathroom paint, 19
border designs, *14*
borders, 35
bright ideas:
  colour washing, 43
  decoupage, 61
  distressing and crackle glaze, 44
  painted furniture, 53
  painting floors, 55
  painting textured wallcoverings, 56-7
  sponging and ragging, 41
  stencilling, 49
  stripes and checks, 51
  wallpaper borders, 59
brushes, 67
bucket, 64

C

ceilings, painting, 68
ceilings, wallpapering, 74
check patterns, *11*
checked wall, *48*
chequerboard pattern on floor, *54*
cleaning brushes, 70
cloth, clean, 67
colour moods, 14-15
colour, playing safe with, 15
colour washing, 21, 42-3, *43*
  bright ideas, 43
colour, working with, 14-15
colours, choosing, 14
crackle glaze, 22, 45
  bright ideas, 44

D

decorative paint effects, 38-9
découpage, 60-1
  bright ideas, 61
découpaged room, *61*

distressed chair, *53*
distressing, 22, 44, *44*
  bright ideas, 44
dragging, 41
dust sheets, 64

E

existing furnishings, 13

F

filler, 64
filling cracks, 65, *65*
filling knives, 64
finishing touches, 34-5
floor, chequerboard pattern, *54*
floral prints, *16*
floral wallpaper, *28*
  designs, 28-9
foamed vinyl, 27
function of room, 12
furniture, painted, 25

G

glazes, 39

H

hanging borders, 75
hanging wallpaper, 72-3

I

inspiration, finding, 10-11

K

kitchen paint, 19

L

lining paper, 27, 72
liquid gloss, 19

M

marbling, 22, 46-7, *47*
  practical pointers, 47
masking tape, 67
mid-sheen oil-based paint, 19

N

new plastered walls, preparing, 65
new woodwork, preparing, 66
non-drip gloss, 19

P

paint:
  applying, 67
  choosing, 18-19
  stripping, 66
  types of, 18
paint effects, decorative, 21-3
  know-how, 39
  what's what, 21-3
paint effect wallpapers, 30
paint patterns, *22*
paint roller, 67
paint stripping material, 64
paint tray, 67
paint versus wallpaper, 17
paintbrushes, cleaning, 70
  dry wide, 64
  painting with, 68
painted details, 24-5, *24-5*
painted floors, 54-5
  bright ideas, 55
painted furniture, 52-3
  bright ideas, 53
painted stripes, *36-7*
painted walls, preparing, 65
painting, 67-70
  ceilings and walls, 68
  equipment, what's what, 67
  practical pointers, 70
  radiators, 70
  textured wallcoverings, 56-7
  with a brush, 68
  with a roller, 68
  woodwork, 69
paints, what's what, 19
panels, *16*
paper-backed vinyl, 27
pattern, working with, 16-17
planning, 10-11
plastered walls, painting newly, 19
practical pointers:
  choosing paint, 19
  hanging wallpaper borders, 75
  marbling, 47
  paint effects, 23
  painting, 70
  painting textured wallcoverings, 57
planning your scheme, 11

preparing surfaces, 64
stripes and checks, 51
wallpaper borders, 59
wallpapering, 71
working with colour, 15
working with pattern, 17
preparation tools, what's what, 64
preparing surfaces for decoration, 64-6
practical pointers, 64
preparing walls, 65-6
primer, 19
print room, *61*

R
radiators, painting, 70
    preparing, 66
rag-rolled pattern, *31, 38-9*
ragging, 21, 41
    bright ideas, 41
relief patterned wallpaper, *12*, 27, *32, 33, 56*
right scheme for right room, 12-13
roller, painting with, 68
room size, 12
room function, 12

S
sandpapers, 64
scrapers, 64
scumble-glaze, 39
self-undercoating gloss, 19
shavehooks, 64
simple patterns, 21
size of room, 12
small wallpaper patterns, 30-1, *30*
solid emulsion/roller paint, 19
sponge, 64
sponging, 21, *23*, 40-1, *40-1*
    bright ideas, 41
stencilled border, *48-9*
stencilled walls, *48*
stencilling, *23*, 48-9
    bright ideas, 49
stencils, 22
step ladders, 64, 67
stippling, 41
striped wall, *48*
striped wallpaper, 31
stripes, *16*, 30

and checks, 50-1
    and checks, bright ideas, 51
    and checks, practical pointers, 51
    painted, *36-7*
stripping paint, 66
style, finding a, 11
style, researching, 11

T
textured wallcovering, painting, 56-7
thinned oil-paint glaze, 39
traditional style wallpapers, 32-3
trompe l'oeil, 23

U
undercoat, 19

V
vinyl-coated wallpaper, 27
vinyl matt emulsion paint, 19
vinyl silk emulsion paint, 19

W
wallpaper, hanging, 72-3
wallpaper borders, *34-5*, 58-9, *59*
    bright ideas, 59
    hanging, 75
        practical pointers, 75
    position of, 58
    practical pointers, 59
wallpaper, what's what, 27
wallpapered walls, 65
wallpapering, 71-5
    calculating the amount of wallpaper needed, 71
    ceilings, 74
    choosing, 26-7
    pointers, 71
wallpapers and borders, coordinating, *10*
walls, painted, 25
walls, painting, 68
walls, problem areas with, 66
washable wallpaper, 27
water-based glaze, 39
what's what:
    paint effects, 21-3
    painting equipment, 67
    preparation tools, 64

types of paint, 19
wallpapers, 27
woodchip, 27
woodwork:
    painted, 24
    painting, 69
    preparing, 66

ACKNOWLEDGMENTS

The author and publisher would like to thank the following companies and people for their help with supplying photographs for this book:

Front cover: (main) HB/Trevor Richards; Ramm Son and Crocker; Dulux Paints; HB/Fototheme; Andrea Cameron. Back cover: HB/Spike Powell.

Page 3, Anaglypta wallcoverings; page 4, Sanderson; page 6, HB/Spike Powell; pages 8-9, Sanderson; page 10, HB/Fototheme; page 11, Sanderson; page 12, The Shaker Shop/Lara Grylls PR; page 13, HB/Trevor Richards; page 14, HB/Ian Parry; page 15, HB/Spike Powell; page 16, Dulux Paints; page 17, Coloroll/Camron PR; page 18, Crown Paints; page 20, Crown Paints; page 21, HB/Tracey Orme; page 22, HB/Ian Parry and Sanderson; page 23, The Stencil Store Company Ltd and Crown Paints; page 24, HB/Tracey Orme; page 25, Crown Paints; page 26, Sanderson; page 28, HB/Derek Lomas; page 29, HB/Steve Hawkins and HB/Ian Parry; page 30, Sanderson; page 31, HB/Dominic Blackmore and Sanderson; page 32, Anaglypta wallcoverings; page 33, HB/Dominic Blackmore; page 37, HB/Trevor Richards; page 38, HB/Ian Kalinowski; page 40, Dulux Paints; page 42, HB/Tracey Orme; page 43, HB/Lizzie Orme; page 44, HB/Derek Lomas; page 45, The Stencil Store Company Ltd; page 48, The Stencil Library; page 49, The Stencil Store Company Ltd; page 50, Crown Paints; page 52, Dulux Paints; page 53, Crown Paints; page 54, HB/Trevor Richards; page 56, Anaglypta Wallcoverings; page 59, Coloroll; page 60, HB/Dominic Blackmore; page 62, Do It All; page 74, HB/Dominic Blackmore.